Dr. Bottaro's work on Catholic mindfulness is a practical application of deep theological teachings from the works of St. John of the Cross and St. Augustine. Mindfulness, through this lens, continually leads and connects us to the reality of the indwelling life of the Trinity, as well as being made in the image of God, with our faculties—when present to Love—moving us toward the Good.

—MOTHER MARY ELIZABETH OF THE TRINITY, OCD
Sub-Prioress of the Carmel of Mary Immaculate
and St. Mary Magdalen

We all long for peace, healing and transformation—emotionally, spiritually, and physically. Dr. Bottaro's informative, creative, and practical presentation of mindfulness through the lens of the Christian mystical tradition offers an authentic spiritual path for Christians who may be wary of a spiritual practice originating from Buddhism. *The Mindful Catholic: Finding God One Moment at a Time* is a welcome and important contribution to the vast literature on mindfulness meditation and the possibilities it offers for personal and collective transformation in Christ.

—FR. DANIEL CHOWNING, OCD
Definitor, General Curia of the Teresian Carmel

PRAISE FOR *THE MINDFUL CATHOL*

Through his insightful exploration of the principle of
mindfulness, Dr. Bottaro has given his readers a powerfu
tool to grow in psychological and spiritual health. This boc
will be of tremendous benefit for anyone who wishes to
develop healthy, joyful, and holy relationships, beginning
with our personal relationship with the Lord Jesus.

—MOST REVEREND FRANK J. CAGGIANO
Bishop of Bridgeport, Connecticut

This is an outstanding and timely book. If people follow i
program many psychologists will be out of work.

—PAUL VITZ, PhD
Author and professor at the Institute for
the Psychological Sciences

The Mindful Catholic is a beautiful expression of how to liv
in the intimacy of a relationship with the Father who love
us. I've known and trusted Greg Bottaro for many years–
first as a student of mine and, now, as a teacher from who
I'm learning. This wonderful integration of timeless trutl
with modern psychology can help us all live more peacefu
in the trust that God calls us to.

—CHRISTOPHER WEST
Author of *Theology of the Body for Beginners*

Spending too much mind time in the past or future lea
to distressing emotions and self-defeating behavior.
Dr. Bottaro teaches how to live in the present, the now
life, for our benefit and that of those we love.

—DR. RAY GUARENDI
Author of *Advice Worth Ignoring*

THE MINDFUL CATHOLIC

FINDING GOD ONE MOMENT AT A TIME

THE
MINDFUL
CATHOLIC

FINDING GOD ONE MOMENT AT A TIME

DR. GREGORY BOTTARO

WELLSPRING

North Palm Beach, Florida

Published by Wellspring

Originally Published by Beacon Publishing

Design by Madeline Harris

ISBN: 978-1-63582-017-1 (hardcover)
ISBN: 978-1-929266-46-3 (e-book)

Library of Congress Cataloging-in-Publication Data
Names: Bottaro, Gregory, author. Title: The Mindful Catholic: finding God one
moment at a time / Dr. Gregory Bottaro. Description: North Palm Beach, Florida:
Beacon Publishing, 2018. Identifiers: LCCN 2017052404 | ISBN 9781635820171
(hardcover) | ISBN 9780984131853 (softcover) | ISBN 9781929266463 (e-book) Subjects:
LCSH: Spirituality—Catholic Church. | Spiritual life—Catholic Church. | Mindfulness
(Psychology) | Attention—Religious aspects—Catholic Church. | Awareness—Religious
aspects—Christianity. Classification: LCC BX2350.3 .B674 2018 |
DDC 248.4/82—dc23

For more information on this title or other books and CDs available through the
Dynamic Catholic Book Program, please visit www.DynamicCatholic.com.

The Dynamic Catholic Institute
5081 Olympic Blvd • Erlanger • Kentucky • 41018
Phone: 1-859-980-7900
Email: info@DynamicCatholic.com

10   9   8   7   6

Printed in the United States of America

*For Fr. Benedict Groeschel, who taught me how
to live in the moment.*

*For my wife, who is teaching me how
to love in the moment.*

"Therefore I tell you, do not be anxious about your life, what you shall eat or what you shall drink, nor about your body, what you shall put on. Is not life more than food, and the body more than clothing? Look at the birds of the air: they neither sow nor reap nor gather into barns, and yet your heavenly Father feeds them. Are you not of more value than they? And which of you by being anxious can add one cubit to his span of life? And why are you anxious about clothing? Consider the lilies of the field, how they grow; they neither toil nor spin; yet I tell you, even Solomon in all his glory was not arrayed like one of these. But if God so clothes the grass of the field, which today is alive and tomorrow is thrown into the oven, will he not much more clothe you, O men of little faith? Therefore do not be anxious, saying, 'What shall we eat?' or 'What shall we drink?' or 'What shall we wear?' For the Gentiles seek all these things; and your heavenly Father knows that you need them all. But seek first his kingdom and his righteousness, and all these things shall be yours as well. Therefore do not be anxious about tomorrow, for tomorrow will be anxious for itself. Let the day's own trouble be sufficient for the day."

—*Matthew 6:25–34*

"One way of easily recalling the mind during prayer and keeping it at rest is not to let it wander during the day. You should keep it strictly in the presence of God; and being accustomed to thinking of Him often, it will be easy to keep your mind under control during your prayers at least to keep it from wandering."

—*Br. Lawrence of the Resurrection*

TABLE OF CONTENTS

FOREWORD

Peter Kreeft

Greg Bottaro was a student of mine at Boston College. He was a very good student, but even very good students seldom write very good books. He did.

It is a good book not just because it reads well but because it works well. This book is like a cookbook, or an instruction manual. To say that it makes a pretty good read is like saying that *How to Build a Boat* makes a pretty good read for a castaway. It does indeed make a pretty good read, but it makes a much better boat. It floats. It works.

And "you're gonna need a bigger boat" is true of all of us in terms of mindfulness. St. Augustine prayed, "Narrow is the mansion of my soul. Enlarge it." The mind is one of the two most essential powers of the soul (the other being the will). What this book does to your mind is not to fill it with stuff but to enlarge it, to strengthen it. It does to the mind what new batteries do to a searchlight.

But you have to *do* it, not just think about doing it. Many of us, especially we academic types, we "intellectuals," who usually have very active imaginations, are prone to think (subconsciously) that we have actually done something (like prayer or fasting or acts of charity) simply because we have thought about it. We can even come to believe that we are saintly simply because we love to read books by the saints. We are tempted to live in our imaginations, in our world rather than in the real world. (It's much easier!) We're like the theologian who, upon dying, was offered by

God the choice between going to heaven and going to a theology lecture on heaven. He chose the lecture.

How important is mindfulness? More important than almost any possible *object* of mind. There are many, many different objects in this crazy, wonderful world for the light of our minds to light up, but if the light is weak or foggy or unreliable, *all* its objects will be dim, and our grasp of them weak, and our very selves dim and weak like ghosts. Our mind can be compared to the light, and everything in our world is an object to it. To improve the light itself—to clarify it and intensify it and focus it and master it—is more important than to know any of its objects (except God and yourself, the only two realities you can never escape for a single moment, in time or in eternity).

Buddha famously said, in the first and most famous and favorite line in the first and most famous and favorite Buddhist book, the *Dhammapada*, "All that we are is a result of what we have thought. It begins with our thoughts, it moves with our thoughts, it ends with our thoughts."

(By the way, this is not a Buddhist book. It is a Christian and Catholic book. It does not lead you into nothingness or emptiness but into everything—especially into God.)

I have ADD (which for a philosopher is usually ADHD, Attention Deficit High Definition); I am easily bored and distracted, so I love short, simple books. If a book makes ten points I will forget nine of them. That's why my favorite spiritual classic is Brother Lawrence's simple little one-point book, *The Practice of the Presence of God*. Its point is so clear and short that even if he never wrote the book, the title alone would be sufficient. Dr. Bottaro's book gives you much more concrete detail, exercises, and specific practical advice, but that's what it all comes down to.

St. Paul knew the importance of thought as well as Buddha did. He tells us to "take every thought captive to obey Christ" (2 Corinthians 10:5). Adam's and Eve's act-sin began with thought-sin. ("Did God really say that? Listen to what I say.") "Sow a thought, reap an act; sow an act, reap a habit; sow a habit, reap a character; sow a character, reap a destiny."

Thought has two poles: the object and the subject, the thing thought about and the act of thought itself. Of course it's important what we think about, what concepts we use, what understandings and beliefs and principles we have in our minds, what objects we focus on. But it's also important, and terribly neglected, to be mindful—i.e., full of mind, full of alpha waves, alert, aware, awake.

This is triply important in an age and a culture that foster a confusing and crippling complexity, a dazzling disarray of diversions, and an always-advancing avalanche of anxieties. Ray Bradbury, in his classic *The Martian Chronicles*, tells a story about an anxious-to-please Martian who is an empath; he gives portions of his mind to every need of every human invader from earth, and finally his mind simply bursts, like an overinflated tire. Too many of us are close to that breaking point. How can we simplify our lives?

That is always a good thing to do with external clutter, but an even better thing to do is to simplify and collect ourselves—i.e., our minds. This book will actually help you to do that.

But it's not a typical pop psychology self-help book. For one thing, it's solidly Catholic. For another thing, it really is simple. There are too many books that give you complex ways to be simple: Twelve Step programs, yogas, noble eightfold paths, zazen, or theories such as personality road maps. One searcher said, "I ran around and around and tried everything, and my mind was like a yo-yo flying centrifugally farther and farther from itself at the end of the string in my very search for the hand that held the string. I tried 'centering prayer,' but it just gave me another thing to run around searching for." Another searcher said, "I tried a Freudian psychologist, but I ended up feeling guilty about one more thing: feeling guilty. I read that 'we have nothing to fear but fear itself,' but that gave me one more thing to fear."

Here is a way out of the hall of mirrors and into the open air, out of the spider web and into the sky.

"The sky" is not an accidental image. This book will help you to pray. It will train you to focus (by this-worldly and sensory imaginative exercises), and thus to focus on God. (You can't focus on God if you can't focus.) And what could possibly be more valuable than that? Prayer is like an oxygen tank to lungs underwater, like electricity to an appliance, like love to a marriage, like food and water to a starving body, like fertilizer to crops.

Try it. You'll like it.

—Peter Kreeft

INTRODUCTION

Living Your Faith

Perhaps this is only my own experience and other people do not find it so. But, speaking for myself, I sometimes long to die because I cannot cure this wandering of the mind.
—St. Teresa of Ávila

The moment one learns to doubt, difficulties begin. The Garden of Eden was paradise until the slimy serpent planted seeds of doubt in Adam's and Eve's minds. Our lives begin without much complication until we start to worry if everything is really going to be OK. The human experience is fraught with a multitude of problems that in many ways stem from doubt.

Have you ever had a restless night of really bad sleep? Racing thoughts can keep anyone awake. It seems like your mind is able to handle the day fairly well, but as soon as the lights go out and your head hits the pillow, your brain gets fired up when all is quiet and still, and your mind gets to work. Thoughts come as if from nowhere. Despite your best efforts, you can't make them go away. You might try turning over, getting up to use the bathroom, putting on a noise machine, or taking some cocktail of herbs and supplements. Yet there they are, as soon as you settle down again, firing up once more and ready to force your attention to keep them company through the midnight hours.

Maybe you've had the experience of driving to work or school, or riding on a bus or train, to find yourself surprised when you get to your destination. "Oh wow, we're here already," you think. In a moment you realize that you were not paying attention to the trip. If you were driving, you might wonder if you stopped at a certain stop sign, or how you managed to turn right or left where you were supposed to if you were not paying attention. Your confusion only grows as you try to remember and nothing comes to mind.

How many times have you been in church listening to the priest give a homily, only to realize that you can't remember what the Gospel reading was about? It isn't rare for my wife to ask me what I thought about the homily and, to my embarrassment, I tell her I don't remember a single word of it—even if we are just walking out of Mass!

Have you ever prayed a Rosary, only to get to the third decade and think to yourself, *Which mysteries are we praying today?* I have.

Whether we are carrying out routine life behaviors, trying to pray, or even in conversation with others, the way our minds work significantly impacts how well we function. God made you for greatness, and he made your mind so that you can use it to achieve that greatness. Most people are living their lives without realizing they are missing so much. This book is all about gaining control of your mind so that you can use it to your best advantage and live up to your highest potential. You will discover truths about the way God created your mind, and the ways it can be held back. You will also discover ways to bring your mind back to a place of optimal functioning and experience the life-changing way that being more fully alive brings peace and joy. Most people are, in many ways, walking around asleep in their lives. You can wake up, and you can be freed from the traps that your mind leads you into.

Our minds wander because we are trying to get ahead of the fact that things are not always OK. At the most primal level, this is because we doubt. Christianity, however, offers the solution. Jesus is our hope, and to believe in him is to believe that all will be well. God provides assurance that we don't need to doubt. Trusting him is the antidote to doubt, and trust is the foundation of our faith. When we trust God and his promises, we enter into a relationship with the Father that is destined for eternal union. Along the way, this relationship means growing every day in peace, letting go of doubt, and accepting all aspects of life as manifestations of God's will.

This book is based on the integration of four decades of scientific research with thousands of years of Catholic spirituality. Since we are created as a union of body and spirit, it makes sense that what is good for our spiritual lives is also good for our bodies. In terms of the science, the parallel discoveries about what is healthy for the mind and body will be introduced to you here. These discoveries actually began as a program to treat chronic pain, which now has matured into a robust form of treatment used to help people find relief from anxiety, depression, eating disorders, addiction, insomnia, scrupulosity, anger, marital difficulties, parenting difficulties, spiritual difficulties, and a host of other problems. These are proven treatment protocols that people use to overcome normal stress, anxiety, exhaustion, and even depression. Those ideas are part of what is called "mindfulness."

Mindfulness

A definition of *mindfulness* that we can work with is "paying attention to the present moment without judgment or criticism." It is a way to be aware with acceptance. It can also be understood as coming to our senses, or very simply, waking up. Mindfulness helps us to become aware of the workings of our minds in a new way. We learn to see just how easily our minds are distracted from the present moment, and how much our avoidance of discomfort actually hurts us.

We are created in the image of God, who is the infinite epitome of mindfulness. If mindfulness is awareness of the present moment, God *is* the present moment. He defined himself as "I am who am." God sees all as a present moment, and it is our goal to see as he sees. We will never see all as he does, but we can see what we see with the light of the present moment.

Here's my proposal: I want to invite you to explore an idea here that has the power to change your life. Since we are made in God's image, we are his children, destined to be like him. We operate at our best—body, mind, and spirit—when we claim our heritage and live according to this nature. Trusting God is the foundation for living this way. When we trust God, we know that all will be well. We see with his kind of eyes, which means that even if we don't know what is about to happen or why, we know that all will be well. This security allows us to fully live in each moment, with all of our capabilities. It allows us to learn from our missteps, accept others in theirs, and grow into the man or woman that God created us to be. In a sentence, it is the real path to holiness and happiness.

You will learn how to be with whatever is happening at the moment, without letting the negative aspects of life overwhelm you. Mindfulness practice has been consistently shown to bring about long-term changes in levels of happiness and well-being. It not only prevents depression but also diffuses the power of stress, anxiety, irritability, and impatience by allowing us to stop the cycles that those emotions typically ignite. Mindfulness was originally used, to great success, to treat chronic pain. In fact, the latest research shows mindfulness having an effect equal to—or in some cases *better* than—morphine to treat chronic pain. It has also been shown clinically to cut the rate of depression by 50 percent for those suffering major depressive disorder. It is quickly becoming a preferred form of treatment, at the very least to accompany antidepressant medication and in many cases instead of it. *Catholic* mindfulness, then, grounds all of this research and practice in a context that goes beyond the psychology.

The underlying brain patterns that are improved with mindfulness also correlate to greater creativity, better memory, and faster reaction times. Have you ever known someone who is very quick-witted? Chances are he or she is tuned in to the present moment.

Are you living up to your greatest potential? Are you as happy as you could possibly be? Most people experience a mix of happiness and frustration, anxiety, sadness, or anger. That is certainly the human condition, and I'm not proposing a way of eliminating all suffering. I am inviting you, though, to go deeper in your understanding of the way God created us. By doing so, you will discover an untapped wellspring of peace and potential.

Our lives are meant to be a journey of continual renewal, or conversion. Even when we've lived through a lot, we can still grow more. One of the most humbling experiences I've had in my life is teaching mindfulness to others. Every time I present the course, and every time I walk this journey with someone, I am reminded of all the ways that I need to grow in being more present and less avoidant of discomfort in my life. I am reminded how much more I need to grow in my trust in God's love and care for me.

There are daily temptations to fall back away from the reality of God's love and be pulled once again into the frantic race of life. Unless you are a monk spending many hours in recollection each day (and monks face the same struggle), the obligations of life tear you away from a sense of inner peace. Add to that the physiological reality of hormonal activity and fluctuating moods, and you end up with a very colorful array of human experience.

These fluctuations are a part of being human by God's design. A "bad mood" might be a kind of alarm that our body is in need of something or we need to change something. Later in the book we will look at ways our emotional life communicates God's will to us (the overlap of Catholic mindfulness with the Spiritual Exercises of St. Ignatius and Discernment of Spirits), but before being able to read those movements of the heart, we need to learn how to stop them from being amplified into something else. A simple bad mood can quickly turn into a bad morning, a bad day, or a bad week! It is our patterns of thinking that turn an anxious moment into an anxiety disorder, or an empty stomach into a bout of depression. These might seem like overly simplistic conceptualizations, but our thinking does lie deeply at the core of many disorders.

Scientific research, especially aided by brain-imaging technology, has made significant discoveries regarding these patterns of thinking, their effect on the brain, and the brain's effect on behavior and lived experience. The first principle that research has taught us is that it is not negative emotion itself that leads the brain toward damaging patterns but *the way we respond to it*. Second, when we try to think our way out of those negative patterns, by either figuring them out or trying to force them out of our minds, we typically make the negative effect worse. For many people, especially those without the guidance of a trained professional, trying to think their way out of a problem in their mind is like trying to swim their way out of quicksand. The more they move, the deeper they sink. The more they think, the worse it gets.

These discoveries shine a bright light on just why it is that we end up in such frantic cycles and patterns of thinking. When we are in a bad mood, unhappy, irritable, or anxious, we usually try to *figure out what the problem is*. As you will come to see, judging that there is a problem is one of the biggest problems! The more we try to figure things out, the more our tendencies of thinking sink our mood. We quickly start to think of how our mood is going to hurt us in parts of our life; we call to mind ways we've gone wrong before, ways we've created problems for ourselves, or ways that other people have been the cause of problems. The more we sit with those thoughts, the angrier, sadder, or more anxious we can get. Then we notice our mood worsening, and we ramp up the effort, trying even harder to figure our way out of it.

Deep down under all that noise can be a quieter voice criticizing you for not being good enough, for not having figured it out yet, and even for not having more hope. Eventually this cycle can end in despair when it's at its worst.

One of my students, Sandra, shared a story about how she'd lost her job. She'd worked at a local bakery and was responsible for ordering inventory. Over the course of three months, a few difficult events occurred. Her husband had been on medication for depression but decided to stop taking it because he was feeling better. His mental state declined in a few weeks and he was irritable and snapping at Sandra over the smallest things. She tried to be patient with him but found herself lying in bed at night wondering how to get through to him and how long she was going to be able to take it. Then her son, who was in college, decided that pursuing extracurricular activities on campus was more important than attending classes, to the point that he was failing most of them, so he decided to simply drop them all and move back home. Sandra knew she couldn't enable his behavior for long, but she also wanted to give him space to figure out what he needed to do to get to a better place. A few weeks after her son came back home, one of her closest friends died in a tragic car accident on a Saturday afternoon as she was on her way to meet Sandra for coffee. Sandra was devastated and fell into a deep rut of self-blame and depression.

She began to lose sleep as she lay awake in bed ruminating about her husband, her son, and her friend. She first blamed her husband and his irresponsibility for everything. He was the reason their son had no drive, and if it weren't for these issues she probably wouldn't have felt the need to meet her friend for coffee that day. Then she started to consider the part she played in her marriage difficulties and beat herself up for not supporting her husband enough years ago when he had really needed it, before he was on medication. She saw how her own imperfections affected everything and she thought to herself, "If only I hadn't been the way I was." She kept thinking this way and felt terrible about who she was then and now, as she continued to lose sleep and deteriorate during the daytime. She started to get more anxious about little things around the house, such as making sure all the doors were locked and reminding her son four or five times a day to always wear his seat belt in the car. At work she was distracted and made several critical errors that cost the business a substantial amount of money. Eventually her inability to do her work led to her termination.

Notice how these difficulties in her life planted seeds of doubt and despair in her mind. As she continued to let them sprout and grow, they took over everywhere else in her life. We don't always have the perfect storm of such difficult circumstances coming together at once, but it is a common thing to let some difficult moment or event turn over in our minds until it becomes something much bigger and much worse.

The practice of mindfulness, especially as it is presented here, integrated with a trust in God, will help you let the moments be moments, and not turn them into more than they need to be. You will learn that those moments do not have to be avoided, and that there really is nothing to fear. Paying attention to the full scope of your life will give you a greater sense of freedom, joy, and peace.

About Your Teacher

I'll share a little about me before we embark on this journey together. I began to practice the basics of mindfulness as a Franciscan friar. In between college and graduate school, I took a bit of a detour from my academic path to discern a religious vocation. I joined the Franciscan Friars of the Renewal in New York City at a time when I was trying to figure out exactly what I wanted to do with my life. There was some turmoil during this process as the difficulties I experienced regarding my parents' divorce caused some confusion about what I was meant to do.

I learned a form of spirituality called Abandonment to Divine Providence from Fr. Benedict Groeschel, and he helped me understand how to let go of all my own unhealthy attachments (and wounds) and trust that God is a good Father who loves us and has a plan for us. Besides being a psychologist, Fr. Benedict was a very holy and mindful man. He was almost constantly in the present moment, unscathed by normal disruptions to plans or expectations. I sought to understand his way of praying and spent hours with the writings of St. Francis, Fr. Jean-Pierre de Caussade, Brother Lawrence, St. Thérèse of Lisieux, St. Elizabeth of the Trinity, and Padre Pio. These saints all wrote extensively about the present moment and abandoning one's trust to God's providential love. I found great peace in this particular spirituality, and it is the way I understand my journey to God. Praying this way helped me to find healing in my own life and see the beauty that God was calling me to in marriage.

Once I left the friars, I enrolled at the Institute for the Psychological Sciences, a graduate program in clinical psychology that integrates sound Catholic philosophy and theology. I had been studying the anthropology of St. John Paul II since college, so this seemed like the only option that made sense for practicing psychology. Five years later I graduated, moved to New York, got married, and started my practice, as well as a family.

Early on I discovered that the way I learned how to pray and discern as a friar informed the way I led my patients in therapy. A colleague introduced me to mindfulness as an empirically validated protocol for treating many types of disorders, and the more I looked into it, the more it resonated with the way I had been coming to know God. Bringing the two together was a perfect match and proved very effective for helping my patients deal with a multitude of diagnoses. For the past four years I have been developing the integration of Catholic spirituality with mindfulness that you will learn about here.

The Approach of This Book

Part of this book is based on an eight-week program called Mindfulness-Based Stress Reduction. Because a typical mindfulness course is given over eight weeks, this book is written with eight chapters that roughly coincide with what is taught in a normal eight-week mindfulness program. You can certainly read through the book at your own pace, or decide to take one chapter per week. You may also choose to read through the book once and then come back to focus and meditate on one chapter per week. However you approach it, you will be given a number of opportunities throughout these chapters to challenge the mental patterns you've developed over the course of your life. You may choose to keep some and change others, but you will have that choice because you'll be aware of those patterns in a way you weren't before.

There are two parts to learning about Catholic mindfulness. First there is the educational aspect. You will learn a lot about the way God made your mind, and the effect your thinking has on your mind and your brain. This educational aspect of mindfulness will help give you a greater understanding of what you are doing when you practice mindfulness and why you are doing it. You will also be learning many ways that our spirituality intersects with our psychology, as well as how much our thoughts and feelings affect our spirituality.

Second, you will have exercises you can practice every day. These practices range from three to twenty minutes. Research suggests that the dramatic effect of mindfulness training over the course of eight weeks is *dose dependent*, meaning the more time you spend learning about mindfulness and practicing the exercises, the more you will experience the effect. I can almost guarantee that when you get to the end of this book, because of the time you will have cumulatively spent practicing the exercises, you will feel more of the effect of the practice and want to start over again to devote more time from the beginning. Most people start reading the book again once they finish. The exercises will be presented for you here in this book, and they are also available to download or stream for free at www.catholicmindfulness.com/audio.

I encourage you to give these exercises a shot. Before deciding to commit to a whole eight weeks, you may do a bit of a test run. Commit to ten days to start. Take the exercise from the first chapter and for the next ten days schedule just ten minutes to sit and practice. I think you'll discover that it is definitely worth your time. As you get going, it is recommended that you practice the exercise of the week at least five days out of seven. Give yourself the best opportunity to wake up from the unconscious patterns of self-sabotage you employ with your mind. Also, it is better to take your time rather than rush ahead. If you find there are a few days that go by when you can't do even one practice, postpone moving ahead and give yourself a few extra days to try again.

Since the spiritual, mental, and physical facets of our humanity are united, there is a physical correlation to the mental states that we experience. Mindfulness not only changes our mental state, it changes our brains. If you took a picture of your brain right now and then practiced mindfulness for eight weeks, the pictures of your brain in eight weeks would look very different. Study after study shows just how effective these exercises are at changing the structure and function of your brain in a healthy way. Researchers are constantly discovering ways in which the brain and mind relate to each other.

Habit Disrupters

You will also have opportunities to change patterns of behavior you have developed in other parts of your life besides the way you think. Changing unrelated behaviors will help you to change patterns of thought. Throughout the book I will invite you to change something simple in your life. These exercises are called Habit Disrupters. Judgmental and self-critical thoughts can sneak around under the surface and arise from patterns of thinking and acting. By disrupting these patterns, you get to take a closer look at what is going on in your mind, and experience a greater sense of freedom in your life. The more you engage with this material, the more you will benefit from mindfulness practice.

The first four chapters will teach you how to wake up to the real functioning of your mind. You will learn about how it works at the physiological level in the brain as well as the felt experience that correlates with that functioning. As you read these chapters, you may have some aha moments as you make sense of annoying or even destructive mental habits that you've been employing. You will understand just how harmful our current way of life is, and why mindfulness is so important. The patterns of thought that plague you will become clearer and you will understand with greater depth those moments when you are overwhelmed with worry, anxiety, sadness, irritability, anger, frustration, or even despair. The role of self-doubt, self-criticism, and even self-hatred will come into full view. These dispositions can underlie the rest of our thoughts, and so we need to uproot them and view them in the light of truth. Mindfulness is about coming to know ourselves in the light in which God sees us.

In chapters five through eight, we move from awareness to action. You will learn what to do with all this material you just learned. At the heart of it all, you will learn how to see the goodness that God created you with out of his own goodness, and how you can be disposed toward yourself, and then all other people, in a proportionate way to that goodness. This is the heart of mercy, and ultimately mindfulness helps us to experience a deeper sense of mercy.

This book will present you with different ways to think about mindfulness. It might feel like we are covering a number of random topics, but they are actually all very closely related. They are all, in fact, describing essentially the same thing. I will use different images, analogies, and exercises to try to communicate these deeply personal and subjective experiences to you in a way that you can incorporate for yourself. At some point along the way, mindfulness will click for you. When this happens will depend on the way you think, your personality type, and how you relate to the various ways of explaining it. The exercises start to benefit you as soon as you begin to practice them, but the deeper sense of what it is all about might take longer to grasp. I have been practicing mindfulness for more than ten years, and my understanding of the way my mind can exist in the present moment continually deepens.

One of the most common roadblocks I've encountered with people starting this journey is the sense that there isn't enough time to absorb the material or practice the exercises. If you feel this way, you can't afford not to read this book. You'll learn how practicing mindfulness will actually increase the amount of free time you have in your day. It doesn't matter if you are a stay-at-home mom with eight kids or a Wall Street CEO—adding in twenty minutes of mindfulness a day will have exponentially greater rewards. In business terms, the return on investment is extremely high. Children, teenagers, and adults of any age can benefit from this time spent nourishing the mind. You are giving *yourself* highest priority in your life by doing so, not in a selfish way, but in a way of good stewardship. This is how you will fulfill all of your goals—spiritual, personal, relational, or vocational— with your greatest ability. Mindfulness will help you become the man or woman God made you to be.

God made you with the highest dignity possible and with a destiny for greatness, but we can all be tempted at times by the thought that we aren't that good. This sense is at the very root of why our minds turn against us in so many ways. By working through this material, you will encounter those parts of your mind and heart and invite healing into them. I have seen miraculous life transformations because of this.

Here you will learn simple exercises that optimize the way your mind works, and you will experience the mental freedom you need to become the best version of yourself. This book does not pretend to offer a way to avoid suffering or make difficulties disappear. In fact, once you progress further, you will realize just how unmindful that notion is. Most difficulties in life are amplified precisely because we are trying to avoid them. Instead we can turn toward anything and everything that comes our way, with a sense of confidence that all will be well, because we have a God who loves us and makes all things well.

Memory and Emotion

Our memory works in mysterious ways. One thing researchers have figured out, though, is that context plays a huge role in the faculty of memory. If you've ever revisited a place from your past, you will have experienced this. In your normal circumstances, you might have small snapshots of memories that you carry with you. When you travel back to a place from your past, though, walking down a street from your childhood, driving through a town you used to live in, or visiting a favorite vacation spot, suddenly a flood of memories comes back from when you were there before. Even if it was thirty years ago, you will still remember people, names, events, and many other details as if they happened yesterday.

Emotional states can be like those streets you walk down. When you feel a spark of some emotion, it creates an internal context for a host of memories of past thoughts, feelings, and events. Before you know it, a flash of sadness, anger, irritability, anxiety, or any other negative emotion triggers a cascade of memories that increase the negative state. What started off as a flickering emotion ends up as a whole day gone bad—but it doesn't have to.

We can't stop the sparks of emotion. There are many things you will learn about in this book that are outside your control. Thoughts and feelings can come out of nowhere, without any warning and sometimes without any indication of why they showed up. Our mind thinks thoughts the way the heart beats. It's always working, even when we aren't paying attention to it, and we certainly don't want to wish for it to stop. What we can control is our response to those thoughts and feelings. We don't have to let the initial spark of some negative thought or feeling become a trigger for a downward spiral.

The mindfulness exercises you learn here will open up to you a new world of relating to your own thoughts and feelings. You will learn how to see them for what they are, and not respond to them as if they are something else. The simple fact that you have a thought does not mean the thought is true. The simple fact that you have a feeling does not mean the feeling is accurate. Thoughts and feelings happen, but they don't have the authority to lay claim to truth. Just because they happen doesn't mean we have to obey them, respect them, or let our lives be run by them.

In fact, thoughts and feelings are in many ways determined by laws of physics and physiology. This reality can tempt many to believe that science is all that exists and everything is explainable in scientific terms. This is what misleads so many researchers who don't believe in God and see humanity as the random consequence of material evolution. It is actually true that our thoughts and feelings are in many ways predetermined. We can measure the connections between simple laws of physics, biology, chemistry, and overall physiology to understand how thoughts and feelings work. You can receive an injection of a chemical right now and your thoughts and feelings will change—predictably.

Beyond these predetermined relationships and laws of physics and biochemistry, though, there is a spiritual dimension that relates to these material realities. We have a transcendent spirit that has a higher sense of "knowing," not subject entirely to the laws of physics. It is this transcendent part of our humanity that can observe the laws playing out in our thoughts and feelings and make a higher *choice* about what to do with them. Even if we are stuck in a spiral at some level, there is always a higher level where some choice could be made to move one step away from the spiral.

In order to get control of this faculty of choice in the midst of thoughts and feelings that are in many ways determined by external factors, we need to reengage a part of the mind that is mostly devalued and underdeveloped in Western culture. Science requires the analytical mind, and we are very good at using that mind. We are taught from an early age that problem solving, thinking, judging, and planning are capacities to develop and excel at. We are tested at an early age for our ability to think "critically." Critical thinking is an important aspect of the way our minds work, but it is not the only aspect. We have done a tremendous disservice to our own humanity by elevating this element of thinking and devaluing the part of our mind that is simply aware. Einstein is quoted as saying, "The intuitive mind is a sacred gift and the rational mind is a faithful servant. We have created a society that honors the servant and has forgotten the gift."

Apart from the ability to think critically about things, reasoning from one point of data to another, we have been given the ability to know things without really thinking about them. When we hear the sound of a stream passing by, or feel the warmth of the sun, or taste our favorite food, we are much closer to using this part of our mind. A sense of simple, intuitive grasping of some point of reality is one of our abilities that is largely underused.

We want to develop this sensory faculty of open awareness that we have. Judging our experience uses the analytical mind; simply being aware without judging does not.

Mindfulness is *nonjudgmental* awareness of our present moment. This means that we do not engage any kind of judgment when we are practicing mindfulness exercises. Judging can mean being very critical of ourselves or others, frustrated, irritated, or any other negative thought pattern. It can also, however, mean something positive. If you are enjoying a moment simply being aware of it and then the idea enters your mind, "*This is so good,* I don't want it to end," you have made a judgment. Even a positive judgment is a judgment, and something that mindfulness teaches us to disengage from.

We are cultivating an open awareness that enables us to sit with greater clarity and creativity in the midst of any experience—even a difficult one. When there is a situation that requires our judgment, approaching it from a place of mindfulness will help us to make better judgments. As you will see moving through this book, the effects of mindfulness will be far reaching.

Getting Started

Learning how to practice mindfulness in a Catholic context is a way to recognize the dignity God created you with and take care of yourself accordingly. You are taking the time for yourself in order to discover more about yourself and learn how to be more accepting of yourself. Self-awareness is a good thing because it will lead you to discover more about *who God made you to be*. This is going to help you become a better man or woman, a better spouse, parent, sibling, student, neighbor, coworker, and ultimately a better Christian. Your happiness is directly connected to you becoming more of who God made you to be.

I encourage you to take some time and consider if you need to rearrange your schedule a bit as you read through this book to make time for yourself. If you don't take this step, it is likely that along the way, other things will become more important. If you let your day be dictated by whatever feels more important moment by moment, this practice will eventually fall by the wayside and some other fire that needs to be put out will be more important. This book will teach you how to be free from putting out fires and regain control of your life, but you need to set aside the time to learn how to do it. Busy people everywhere know that if it doesn't get scheduled, it doesn't get accomplished.

As you progress, you will find it easier to make time for your exercises. Breaking down old, useless patterns of thinking will help you realize that it was precisely those ways of thinking that zapped all your time. Without awareness of what happens in your mind or body, you repeat the same unhelpful ways of thinking. New ways of thinking will lead to more productivity and a great sense of satisfaction.

It is also helpful to let other people around you know that you are embarking on this journey. It is even better if you have someone to travel with you along this path. Share the book with someone you know and plan on times to discuss it. You can practice mindfulness with others and discuss the experience together.

Even if someone isn't reading the book with you, you can still let people you live with know what you are doing so they can help you protect your time and space to be free from as many distractions as possible. Life happens, and it can all be folded into your mindfulness exercise. Sometimes you might need to attend to those distractions, but more times than not it is only our thoughts that make us believe we need to attend to them. You will learn how to pause and look more deeply at those distractions when they occur.

Here is one last note of preparation before we get started. This is a very important point that I want you to come back to throughout the book. Mindfulness is not easy. It is not academically difficult, but it can be personally challenging. Mindfulness will help you become the man or woman God created you to be. That means conversion, change, and growth. It means learning to see things more like God does, and ultimately trusting his promise that all will be well over the illusion that all will not be well. Those things do not happen without some challenges, difficulties, and failures along the way. You can very easily feel like you are failing as you attempt to practice the exercises, *but it is supposed to be that way*. Through these exercises, you will encounter your own thought process in a new way, and learn how you treat yourself differently. It is in observing yourself as you feel failure that you will break through those thought patterns and learn how to see yourself the way God does. You may be challenged by a sense of boredom, frustration, sleepiness, or simply not having enough time. You will discover that the mind is very resistant to making the changes I am proposing here. It will come up with all kinds of ways to avoid engaging with this material. By learning how to observe these patterns, which are actually present in most of our lives in other areas, you will discover how to defuse their power over you. Awareness is like naming something: As soon as you name it, you are in control of it.

My prayers are with you as you make your way through this book. May the grace of God fill your heart with the peace that he created you for.

EXERCISE

Raisin Exercise

Here's a short exercise to introduce you to mindfulness. To do this, you'll need a small piece of food such as a raisin, a chocolate, or a nut.

- Prepare yourself for this exercise by sitting upright in your chair, taking a deep breath, and focusing for a moment on the breath as it enters your chest. Focus on the sensations of physical touch as your chest expands and as it contracts.

- Place the food in your palm. Look at it as if you have never seen anything like this before.

- Draw your attention to what you see. Look at the food. Let your eyes explore every part of it as you turn it in your hand. Examine the folds and ridges, the different shadows, the colors, the textures. Turn it over and watch as it moves.

- Bring your focus to your sense of touch. Feel the food. Explore its texture between your fingers.

- Now bring it up to hold it under your nose. See what you notice with each in-breath. Does it have a scent? Allow this to fill your awareness. If there is no scent, that is OK. You are simply trying to notice what is here.

- Slowly move the food to your mouth. Gently place it in your mouth, noticing what your tongue does to receive it. Without chewing, simply explore the sensations of having it on your tongue. Gradually explore the food with your tongue and the other parts of your mouth. Roll it around. Feel it. Taste it as if you have never tasted it before. What other sensations are present?

- When you're ready, bite into it. Notice the effects of this object in your mouth. Notice any tastes it may release. Feel the texture as you bite into it. Continue slowly chewing it, but do not swallow it just yet. Notice what is happening in your mouth. Explore these sensations with curiosity, really experiencing what it is like to chew this food.

- While chewing, notice the sensation of swallowing that will start to develop. Notice when that first intention arises. Experience it fully, allowing that intention to swallow to arise in your mind before finally giving in.

- Follow the sensation of swallowing the food, consciously sensing as it moves down your throat into your stomach. Notice a second or a third swallow until it is gone. Notice what your tongue does after you swallow.
- Finally, spend a few minutes registering the aftermath of this eating. Is there an aftertaste? What does the absence of the food feel like? Is there an urge to look for another piece?
- Sit for just a moment and let this sink in.
- Now take a minute and write down anything you noticed while doing this exercise. What stood out to you?

Instead of mindlessly eating handfuls of food, you have intentionally spent this time with one tiny piece and appreciated it with almost all of your senses. You have come to have a greater and deeper experience of eating, actively participating in the process, more fully alive than maybe ever before.

Habit Disrupter: Routines
Choose a simple activity you do every day, such as brushing your teeth or making breakfast. Intentionally pay attention to this activity every day for a week with your five physical senses engaged. For example, when you are brushing your teeth, notice the feeling, sound, smell, taste, and sight of what you are doing for the duration of the activity. Instead of planning what you will wear or thinking about what your kids are doing or your commute to work, just focus on what is happening in the moment. Your mind will wander off to start thinking about something else—as soon

as you recognize that this has happened, gently turn your attention back to some physical aspect of the behavior.

CHAPTER ONE

In the Beginning

Let us come forth and treasure the fleeting moment which alone is ours. Let us not waste time, from one moment to another, because the latter is not yet ours.
—Padre Pio

There was a particularly difficult exam in graduate school that I felt extremely stressed about. After a long night of tossing and turning, imagining how difficult the test was going to be, I woke up feeling exhausted. I stumbled out of bed, made my way to the coffeepot, and turned it on. At that moment I remembered that I also needed to bring in a signed form for a supervisor concerning a patient I was working with. My mind raced as I tried to figure out how best to organize my time getting to school, getting in a few minutes of last-minute studying, and getting the form to my supervisor's office before the test. As my plan was coming together, it hit me that my gas tank was almost empty. Would I have enough gas to get to school? The stop at the gas station was going to cost me an extra fifteen precious minutes! I was rushing around to get ready while the coffee was brewing. There was no time for breakfast, so I started to throw together a smoothie instead. At this point I was frantically hurrying around the kitchen, pulling on socks and throwing fruit into the blender. I went to grab the keys and add an apple to the smoothie when I threw the keys into the blender instead!

After I lost another five minutes cleaning the car keys, I made it to the gas station and then rushed to school. I met a classmate at the door, and she noticed I was quite disheveled. "Are you OK?" she asked.

"Yeah I'm fine," I replied. "But I am not ready for this test!"

She looked at me, confused. "You mean tomorrow's test?"

That was not one of my finer moments. Little did I know I would use it someday to illustrate an aspect of our minds.

The Sympathetic Nervous Response

The body has a very primitive and basic survival instinct built in called the *sympathetic nervous response* (SNR). This is the group of physiological reactions set off by the brain that occur in the face of danger. It is commonly known as the fight-or-flight response, but it is actually more appropriately called the fight-flight-or-freeze response, because freezing up is also one of the survival mechanisms that can be stimulated by this brain response.

The effects of the sympathetic nervous response have to do with the release of epinephrine after a series of reactions that begin in the part of the brain called the amygdala. Cortisol is then released, triggering a number of physiological reactions you feel in your body. Heart rate acceleration, flushed skin, digestion inhibition, dilation or constriction of blood vessels, muscle tightness, and even shaking are all effects of this response. Some or all of these symptoms are commonly associated with stress, frustration, anger, or depression, exhaustion, and despair. You have felt this at times with sweaty palms, tightness in the chest, or feeling hot in the face. A cognitive effect is a narrowing of our field of mental focus. Whatever triggers the response takes center stage in our mental awareness. We become hyperfocused on whatever threat or danger we've perceived.

This last point about cognition is critical in understanding why mindfulness has such an impact on people's lives. If we spend most of our day perceiving danger or problems to react to, we focus on them and lose our perception of other things happening. Since mindfulness ultimately turns down our SNR, it helps us to be aware of more that is happening around or inside us. When my SNR was activated in the middle of the night before my exam, I lost perception of what day it was. This spiraled into the morning, and I kept moving forward without that perception. The cortisol produced by my adrenal glands because of the threat I perceived in the test narrowed my ability to think about what day it was (or where I was putting my keys).

As a result of the sympathetic nervous response, we can sense a threat to our life and have a much better chance of either escaping it or fighting it off. God made us with this bodily phenomenon for a very specific purpose: so we can preserve our life. Thank God! The problem enters when we allow the SNR to be triggered when we aren't actually in danger. This response is primitive because it does not have a complex way of sorting out the differences between real and perceived danger. Perceived danger is actually at the root of most psychological disorders. Some conceptualizations of psychological disease ultimately pin all anxiety-related disorders on the fight-or-flight response, and depressed or mood-related disease on the freeze response. Our systems either speed up or slow down depending on the sympathetic nervous response and its reaction to a perceived threat.

Doing and Being

The easiest way to understand how the SNR works is this: When our brains perceive a problem, a threat, or some kind of danger, they operate as if we are at point A and need to get to point B. Point A represents our current position, the one where this is some problem or danger; point B represents the place where we will be safe, or have a solution to our problem. It takes energy to move from point A to point B, and so the SNR triggers chemical reactions in the brain that move the person between them. We can understand the mind-set in which we need to get from point A to point B as the *doing mode* of mind. When a problem is judged to exist, the brain responds to that judgment in order to move you from the problem of point A to the solution of point B. Again, the brain is not very sophisticated in its judgment of what kind of difficulty point A is. It could be the sound of someone breaking in at night, it could be getting lost on your way to a friend's house, or it could be getting your taxes sorted out. The way we think about the problem is what triggers the brain to perceive a problem, which then triggers the sympathetic nervous response.

The opposite of this brain state happens when we perceive that there is no problem. We decide that point A is OK; there is no need to figure out a point B. This is considered the *being mode* of mind. Being mode is when we are totally safe and there is no problem to solve. We are actually born with a strong tendency to stay in this state, as we are born with a natural inclination toward mindful awareness. Babies haven't yet built up a store of experiences that teach them to fear perceived threats, and so as infants we had a greater ability to experience the world as it was, one moment at a time. You can see what the being mode looks like if you watch a baby discover new things such as his hand or foot. He looks with wonder and explores things with a gentle curiosity.

Curiosity is a fundamentally important concept to understand for mindfulness. You can't be curious and unhappy or stressed at the same time. If you consider your emotional state when you are upset, you will notice that having a sense of curiosity at the same time seems to be out of the question. If you think about times you were curious about something, it is hard to imagine being unhappy at the same time. It seems as though curiosity and unhappiness are antithetical brain states. That's because true, open curiosity points to awareness of what is happening at the moment. When you are aware of the present moment, you are presenting that moment to the brain. It is very rare that at any given time your bodily safety is being threatened. Therefore, if you are curiously aware of whatever is happening at the moment, chances are it is not going to trigger your SNR. Curiosity is a quality of the being mode, in which there is no problem at point A, and point A is OK.

Curiosity, then, is the disposition of mind that we are seeking to cultivate when we practice mindfulness. We want to remain open to experiencing things as they truly are, and not through the filter of our perceptions of danger to flee from or problems to solve. We want to learn how to stay in the being mode of mind, resting in the present moment with the assurance of being safe there.

I was stuck in the doing mode when I woke up stressed over my exam. I immediately perceived a problem that needed to be solved, and so my brain fired off the sympathetic nervous response and got to work solving my problem, or trying to move me from point A, where I was in danger of not doing well on the exam, to point B, where I would do well. My mind hyperfocused on solving the problem, so I didn't notice my keys when I put them in the blender, I didn't notice I needed gas until I was already pressed for time, and most importantly, I didn't notice the day on the calendar and when the exam actually was. Being in the SNR limited my mental capacity. You will learn later how this is also a significant limitation to our capacity for creativity.

Our Brains on Autopilot

My exam story also shows what the mind does on autopilot. We have an amazing tendency to operate at times almost completely by habit. These habits we develop over time are an advantage because of limits in what is called *working memory*. Because my mental capacity was so limited by hyperfocusing on a problem, I was running on habits that had been built into my autopilot. My working memory was totally focused on thoughts running away with themselves about the exam.

Have you ever been working through some mundane task and realized halfway through that you were doing it wrong? Another time in college I was putting laundry into the washing machine. A friend started talking to me, and even though I had already decided to wash whites, had put in the bleach, and had started adding white clothes, I also ended up putting my jeans, colored shirts, and dark socks into the washer. I didn't realize what had happened until my spotted clothes came out.

You might have been driving and ended up taking a turn to a friend's house when you meant to go to the store. You might have gone online to look something up and found yourself going to your email instead. When your email page popped up you thought to yourself, "I just checked email five minutes ago! What was I doing again?" These are all examples of the autopilot mind.

Working memory describes the part of our brain that can handle conscious tasks that we are holding in the forefront of our mind. There is a very small amount of information that we can actually hold in this part of our memory.

Since we can hold only a limited number of things at once in our working memory, we tend to get very frustrated when the memory banks fill up. The more we are expected to accomplish at once, the slower our processing speed gets. It's like opening multiple windows on the computer. If you start too many programs without shutting others down, the computer slows down. If you open too many more, it can even freeze up. Our minds are very similar. We carry out extremely complex operations every moment of the day. Everything our bodies do requires the coordination of thoughts, movements, muscle coordination, and sense coordination. Have you ever watched toddlers learn how to walk? They have to look where to place their feet and figure out what to do with their hands, and they need to consciously work out how to shift their weight. Those first days are a great display of walking via working memory. If all we had was the working memory to get us through the day, there wouldn't be much that we could actually get done because it is so limited.

Little by little, however, the more we accomplish certain tasks, the more these operations move from working memory to autopilot. Autopilot describes the way our minds can accomplish tasks unconsciously. We don't walk like toddlers anymore.

Another example of the autopilot is driving a car with a manual transmission. When people first learn how to drive a stick shift, it can be very awkward. Both feet and both hands are required in a very different way than in driving an automatic transmission. At first, full concentration is required to shift, brake, and accelerate with two feet, and to know when to take one hand off the wheel to move the gearshift. Perfect timing is required to engage the clutch at the correct time. If you've ever learned how to drive a stick shift, you know it's hard to even listen to someone talking while you figure out all this timing and movement.

Slowly over time, you become habituated to these movements, and you need to concentrate less on what you are doing. The way you shift and move your feet feels more comfortable, and before long, you are driving without giving it much thought at all. Whereas before you could hardly tolerate someone talking to you, now you can hold a burger in one hand and a cup in the other, and somehow still manage to steer and shift while carrying on a full conversation with the person next to you. This is because the movements required to drive the stick shift become a part of your autopilot.

The autopilot is a kind of built-in "life hack." It's a way our brains try to save time and energy by grouping together patterns of movement, processes, and even more complex things such as social norms, daily routines, and how to understand other people. If you had to approach each person you met in your day as if it was the first person you'd ever seen in this world, without some understanding of what is meant by tone of voice, the movement of a hand toward you for a handshake, and the meaning behind a certain look, you would spend an hour trying to check out at the grocery store or pump gas.

The autopilot skill we develop throughout our life is a tremendous benefit of being human. We learn as we grow, and certain tasks, jobs, and relationships become easier over time. This tendency, however, can quickly become a deficit if you are unaware of its existence. We build up expectations and move experiences into our autopilots even when they are negative. The habits you develop trigger thoughts, and those thoughts trigger feelings. You may have had a number of bad experiences with customer service people on the phone. After spending countless hours of your life on hold, you developed an expectation that calling anyone for anything is a tedious task. When you see a mistake on a bill you receive, the last thing you want to do is call someone to talk about it. You start to dread the task, and wonder if you can't just let the overcharge go. Maybe it will be worth the $11.43 to not have to waste time on hold *again*. You anticipate an argument with the person who will answer the phone, and having to then wait to speak to a manager. All the while your thoughts are triggering a stress response in your brain, which increases your heart rate and puts you into a state of anxiety.

You might then realize that you are making a bigger deal out of this than is necessary. You start to feel bad about yourself for getting so worked up. You wonder if there's something wrong with you, but then you remember that it's the bill that is wrong, not you! But then you remember all the other times you made a big deal out of something small, and you beat yourself up some more. You try to think your way out of these feelings but it seems to only make it worse.

Thinking your way out of these kinds of situations is like trying to open another computer program to solve the problem of too many programs being open. Instead of engaging with these thoughts and trying to argue your way out of them, it is better to learn how to start closing programs down.

This is the basic beginning to understanding what mindfulness is. Instead of letting your autopilot dictate what you do with your mind, you step outside the process and observe it, then make a choice as to the best way to handle it. You can release yourself from the habits of expectations you have built up over the years and decide what kinds of behaviors to keep in autopilot, such as deciphering the meaning of a handshake, and what kinds of behaviors to try to see differently, like someone rushing past you and nudging you out of the way on the sidewalk. You might be tempted to think that person is acting rude, but it also might be that she just received a call that her loved one is in the hospital.

St. Thérèse wrote, "We should judge our neighbor favorably in every circumstance and make it become a habit of ours to overlook his faults. Just as we—almost spontaneously—give ourselves the benefit of the doubt, let us also make this an integral factor of our relations with those about us." She understood well that (a) we have a tendency to judge the actions of others around us negatively, and (b) this is based on habits that can be changed.

The first step to overriding this autopilot tendency in the places where it works against your goals is to become aware of its existence. In order to become aware of it, start paying more attention to the assumptions your mind makes about ordinary circumstances.

The autopilot is another way to understand the doing mode, and intentional awareness is a way to understand the being mode. Besides the autopilot vs. intentional awareness paradigm, here is a summary of six different ways of understanding the doing mode and the being mode as conceptualized by Mark Williams and Danny Penman in their book, *Mindfulness*.[1] These are all concepts that will continue to be unpacked.

1. **Analyzing vs. Sensing:** Our mind can think, and it can sense. We get so used to living in the world only through

the thinking mind, and we tend to believe the stories that we can make sense of. We've already begun to see how the thinking mind can actually get derailed, and so it is not always the best guide. We have a whole different capacity for sensing, being aware, and simply being open to the things we touch, taste, see, hear, and smell as if for the first time, or the spiritual and emotional movements within us. Living through the sensing mind allows us to rediscover the curiosity that opens us up to our reality in a brand-new way. God made both parts of our mind, and it is essential that we learn how to tap into them. When it comes to discerning the movements of God within us, we need to be able to use both thinking and sensing capacities.

2. **Striving vs. Accepting:** In the doing mode we constantly compare what we perceive in our reality with what we want reality to be. This contrasts with an open perception of reality, in which we allow what we perceive to simply be as it is. When we compare ourselves to what we don't have, we end up miserable. When we take account of what we do have, we find happiness. This is also at the root of gratitude, another concept that is integral to Christian faith and human flourishing.

3. **Thoughts Are Real vs. Mental Events:** When in doing mode, we place implicit trust in the reality of our thoughts. As our frantic minds move through different ruminations, they don't stop to really see the thoughts as they are; instead, they passively and automatically accept that they must be true or valuable because they occurred in our minds. When

in being mode, we see thoughts as mental events that occur in the mind, which either may or may not be true. The being mode suspends judgment of whether the thoughts are true and simply observes what they are, like clouds floating by in the sky as we sit grounded in the present moment.

4. **Avoidance vs. Approaching:** While in doing mode, the mind is trying to avoid a problem. This problem sets up the $A \rightarrow B$ dynamic, which means you need to stimulate the energy (anxiety) to get from A to B. This is the opposite of the being mode, in which the mind has a sense of curiosity about everything going on in this moment, and it doesn't need to move to a place of safety or solution. Approaching is similar to curiosity. We approach our reality in being mode.

5. **Mental Time Travel vs. Present Moment:** Our thoughts change when we are stressed, upset, sad, depressed, angry, or even just feeling a bit behind. Our moods drastically affect the way our minds work. It's as if we are wearing colored dark glasses and everything we look at is tainted by the color. When we remember difficulties from the past, we typically remember things with a negative bias, and when we think of the future, we anticipate things with the same bias. In this kind of mood, we don't at first realize that we are even feeling or thinking this way. We relive the feelings we experienced at those times, or we pre-live the feelings we expect we are going to experience when something negatively slanted happens. This occurs when the doing mode is active and we process those memories or thoughts of the future on autopilot. Being mode does not mean the absence

of thought, or the absence of memories or planning for the future. It means you have part of your mind tuned in to the fact that *at this present moment* you are remembering something from the past or planning something in the future. You don't get lost in those thoughts and detached from being grounded in the present moment, but instead experience memories or anticipation as they really are.

6. **Depleting vs. Nourishing Activities:** When we are in doing mode, it is because there is some goal we are striving for. The brain is not complex in its planning of how to reach goals. It simply executes a way to fix whatever is in its immediate view. It takes a rational person to step in and decide what goals are worth striving for and—this is what this book will help develop—to decide the best way to actually reach those goals. When we are frantically in doing mode, we don't typically think the best thing to do is to pause, take a break, and do something that replenishes us at the deepest level. When we feel frantic because the house is a mess, we think, "If I clean the house, the problem will be solved." Actually, that is not true. If we are racing around on autopilot trying to clean the house, we don't do as good a job as when we do it mindfully aware of what we are actually doing. Taking a few minutes to collect ourselves and then returning to the work at hand will make our work better, and therefore we will accomplish it more efficiently. In this case taking a break is more effective for getting the house cleaned. Most people feel they don't have time for what this book proposes. You should give yourself a lot of credit for getting started here and taking care of yourself in this way.

You will learn that no matter how frantic life seems, taking time out to nourish yourself and make yourself better is the only way to relieve that burden.

You will come to learn that *mindfulness does not mean turning off the thoughts in your mind, but using them as a door to greater awareness of yourself.* This is actually one of the essential differences between Catholic mindfulness and Eastern-based forms of meditation. Many meditative practices seek to *empty* the mind of thought. Hopefully you understand at this point that emptying our minds of anything is not our goal. The very name of this practice is mind*ful*ness. We want to fill our minds with reality. The problems we face in our day are exponentially amplified by allowing ourselves to be dragged into the fantasies created by our imagination. The thoughts that our minds produce are not by nature grounded in truth. We can just as easily have the thought "The sky is green" float through our minds as we can "The sky is blue." Just reading the words puts the thought itself in your mind. There is no gatekeeper that blocks untrue thoughts from passing across the mind-scape. Yet we allow ourselves, without realizing it, to react to each and every thought as if it was true. Mindfulness is not about emptying the mind of thoughts, but it is about seeing thoughts for what they really are.

The most important thing about mindfulness is that you practice it. There is only so far that reading about it will go toward changing the patterns of neuro-behavior in your brain and the way your mind works. The purpose of this book and the classes I teach is to introduce you to the ideas and help you gain greater insight into what is actually happening while you practice. The real core of what will transform your mind, though, is in the practice.

It is possible to change the habits you've unconsciously developed related to your emotions as well. This book teaches you the practical ways you can change the habits of rumination, worry, stress, irritability, anger, judgmentalism, and many other weaknesses that start in the mind. Virtue takes practice, and these exercises will strengthen virtue in the mind and heart.

One student, Theresa, shared her experience as she began to practice mindfulness. She said that in the beginning she was able to practice the exercise twice a day, and had a great mix of feelings about it. At first she was proud of herself for getting started, but as soon as she began her practice, a flood of ideas came to her about all the things she had to get done. "I really have no time for this right now—what was I thinking?" Then she convinced herself to buckle down and stick to the commitment she'd made to herself. A few moments later, she remembered she'd promised she would call her mom. "I forgot about this all day. If I don't do it now, I'll forget again. She's going to be mad at me; she always makes me feel guilty for not calling her. Why can't she realize I have a life? She acts like I don't love her because of a missed phone call." In the midst of this thought stream she realized she hadn't heard the last three minutes of the exercise. Then she wondered if she should start over, or just keep going. She turned away from those thoughts and back to the exercise. Then she thought, "I can't wait until this teaches me how to be free of all these thoughts."

She shared that she felt emptying the mind was the goal at first, despite hearing and reading that wasn't the case. As she progressed, she came to see any of the thoughts that crossed her mind as mental objects. They were simply clouds passing by in the mind-scape, and she could sit like a solid mountain, unmovable no matter what kinds of clouds they were. Some thoughts were like thunderclouds, some with lightning that seemed to threaten her safety. She learned more and more, though, that she could remain like a mountain, unmoved by whatever passed by in the sky. Other days there would be softer, more comfortable clouds floating through, and still she was the solid mountain. We are tempted also to follow pleasant thoughts, to come off our grounding to follow where they go. We must turn away from pleasant or positive thoughts as well. "This is great; I feel so relaxed. Why didn't I do this before?" can quickly turn into "How long will it last?" or "What can I do to make this last?" and then finally, "There's no way this will last. It's only a matter of time before this brief passing relief is gone, and then I'll feel worse because I know what I was missing."

In the beginning especially, the practice of mindfulness is all about learning how to turn our attention where we choose, and for now we choose to turn it away from thoughts. We can acknowledge them, even label them, but then turn away from them, back to the guided practice at hand.

During this time of redirection, it is essential that you are gentle with yourself. It is very easy to be judgmental or critical toward yourself when your thoughts pull you away from the practice. "There I go again." "I'll never get this." "This is no use." Gently escorting our focus back to the practice at hand is far more beneficial to training that focus muscle and helping us attain our bigger goal than beating ourselves up. Pay attention, though, to how you react in those moments of distraction. How you treat yourself during mindfulness practice is a good indication of the deeper feelings and beliefs you carry around about yourself. As we progress, you will come to see that your deeply held beliefs about yourself play a huge role in your ability to know God, to receive his love for you, and to live that love out in your life.

This gentle disposition of self-acceptance is helpful especially during times of prayer. Of the mind in recollection before the presence of God, Br. Lawrence wrote, "If it sometimes wanders and withdraws itself from Him, do not let it upset you; confusion serves rather to distract the mind than to recollect it; the will must bring it back calmly; if you persevere in this way, God will have pity on you."[2] Furthermore, this peaceful acceptance will not only help us in prayer; it is part of the goal of prayer. It is a facet of interior peace that facilitates a deep awareness of the presence of God at all times. In fact, Fr. Jacques Philippe says:

> [O]ne of the most common strategies of the devil in his efforts
> to distance us from God and to slow our spiritual progress is to
> attempt to cause the loss of our interior peace. . . . It would be
> well to keep this in mind, because, quite often in the daily un-
> folding of our Christian life it happens that we fight the wrong
> battle, because we orient our efforts in the wrong direction. . . .
> This is one of the greatest secrets of spiritual combat—to avoid
> fighting the wrong battle.[3]

We cannot win the battle if it requires perfect recollection and focus, or the perfect avoidance of every fault and imperfection. The battle we can win is the one for interior peace that rests on acceptance. This is the peace that God invites you to.

EXERCISE

Mindfulness of Body and Breath

This is a basic exercise to introduce you to some of the principal elements of a mindfulness exercise. Your breath is an anchor that will be revisited often throughout the coming weeks. While there is some spiritual meaning to the breath (Holy Spirit, creation of the world, etc.), the most important thing about the breath for a mindfulness exercise is that it is always with you, and it is always fluctuating. It is generally easier to pay focused attention to things that are moving because they hold your interest a bit more than things that are static. You will develop the ability to focus on static points, but you will always be able to return to the breath.

Pick a consistent time twice a day that generally works for you. It is especially helpful to practice before times of prayer. You can also pray the novena included at the end of the book after one of your practices each day.

- Start off either standing or sitting, allowing your eyes to close. Take a moment to get comfortable, then draw your attention to your breath as you inhale and exhale.
- Call to mind the presence of God and ask him to be here with you now.
- Begin by bringing your awareness to your body, taking in the sensations coming from the points of contact between your body and what is supporting it, whether it's something you are sitting on or standing on. Take a minute now to open to what sensations are present.

- As thoughts come into your mind, let them come. Acknowledge them. Then gently move your focus back to your body and the sensations that are present.
- Try to maintain a disposition of curiosity toward your body, and be open to the sensations that are present. Return your attention to exploring these sensations with curiosity every time you find your mind wandering away to some thought.
- Next, begin to move through the body with your awareness. As you slowly do so, spend about five seconds on each of the following body parts, starting with a narrow focus on the part, then expanding to the whole: your foot (first right, then left), lower leg (right, then left), entire leg (right, then left), then both legs. Move your attention through the chest, back, shoulders, neck, head, and now the whole body.
- Then take a minute to sit with expanded awareness of your whole body at once.
- Bring your awareness to the center of your body; pay attention to the sensations of your breath moving in and out of your body. Stay here for a minute.
- There is no need to control your breath. Just observe and be with your breath as it is. Simply pay attention to what is happening.
- Thoughts may come. This is OK. Be aware of these thoughts as they arise. Then simply, gently escort your focus back to your breath.
- Follow the breath. Pay attention to any and all sensations that may arise from it coming in and out.
- As the exercise comes to an end, call to mind the presence of God once again. He is here with you now. Take a moment and rest with him now.

Habit Disrupter: Changing Your Seat

Think of a place you sit every day that never changes. This could be at home or work, where you sit for a short time or a long time. Change where you sit for a week and see the world from a different perspective. Try this at least once a day.

CHAPTER TWO

The Body Makes Visible the Invisible

Anxiety is the greatest evil that can befall a soul, except sin.
God commands you to pray, but He forbids you to worry.
—St. Francis de Sales

In the previous chapter you were introduced to a new way of understanding your mind and how it works. By learning about the autopilot, you saw that there is a long current of chatter that occurs without you even realizing it. You also learned that it is up to you, once you are aware of this chatter, whether you continue to follow its path or turn away from it. Hopefully you have begun to experience the effect of choosing not to continue to follow it and allowing the chatter to decrease by turning away from it and toward something happening in the physical world in the present moment.

In this chapter you will learn about the effect those thoughts have on your body and the way your body reciprocates feelings to your mind. A patient, we'll call him Adam, learned this at a critical time in his life.

Adam came to see me as a referral from his physician. He became a partner at his firm in his early thirties, and managed a team of twelve. Adam was known for being a family man, he was always available to his team, and he was really good at his job. He motivated his team by his own example, and the other partners had been impressed with him from the beginning.

The past six months had become difficult, though, as the firm faced new regulations to comply with and people were scrambling to make sense of new roles. His sister was diagnosed with lupus, so his family was going through a trial, and the extra work had seemed to pull Adam away from the prayer time he used to make for himself in the mornings, so his spiritual life seemed to be weakening as well.

At first Adam simply felt frantic, rushing around most of the day putting out fires. Eventually he found himself feeling very nervous, and he would need to stop in the restroom a few times a day to splash a little cold water on his face. When he did pause, he noticed his heart was pounding in his chest. Two weeks before he came to see me, the first migraine came back. He hadn't suffered from migraines since college, but he had experienced three in the previous two weeks.

Everyone at work knew Adam was going through something. He was distant in meetings and less excited about everyone else's work. Just the absence of his normal positivity was a heavy weight on the office. His wife knew everything that was going on, and she also knew he was starting to have trouble handling things. She urged him to see his doctor, and he finally agreed. Adam's heart checked out fine, and his physician told him to see a psychologist in order to work through the stress he was feeling, explaining that Adam was being affected by the thoughts and feelings in his mind as much as by the pain and tension in his body.

Feedback Loop

Adam was experiencing the feedback loop that occurs between the brain and the body. The body is very obedient to the commands issued to it by the brain, which is a finely tuned, ultrasensitive instrument that picks up even the tiniest flicker of danger in the mind. If the mind is in doing mode, the brain on autopilot will register any idea of a problem that crosses the mind-scape, and the body will immediately react. Most of this happens outside the reach of conscious awareness, so we don't even realize it is happening. Our body is constantly reacting to the thoughts that register in our mind, if for only a brief second, without our knowing it. The body doesn't stop to consider whether the thought is an actual danger or threat that requires a sympathetic nervous response—it simply reacts.

The loop circles back again when the mind observes what is happening in the body. Adam felt his heart pounding and worried about his health. He started imagining scenarios in which he had a heart attack and left his family abandoned. He imagined what would happen if the firm went under and he didn't know how to start over. He imagined his sister dying and the grief they would all suffer. These thoughts triggered worse feelings in his body and the cycle only continued.

In *Mindfulness*, Williams and Penman cite a study, led by Gary Wells and Richard Petty, that was conducted to show the connection between the mind and body.[4] Participants were asked to rate the sound quality of a pair of headphones based on music and the sound of someone speaking. They wanted to test the sound quality in a "real world" application, so they told one group of participants to move their heads in an up-and-down direction, as if they were looking at the sky while out for a run, and other participants to move their heads back and forth, as if they were turning to see someone while running, or looking before crossing a busy street.

The people who moved their heads up and down while listening to the sound reported better sound quality than the people who moved their heads from side to side while listening to the same sound on the same pair of headphones. Moving their heads in a direction typically associated with saying either yes or no affected the way participants thought about things.

Additionally, the students participating in the research were asked another question on their way out. In a seemingly unrelated survey, they were asked about their opinion regarding college tuition. Increasing tuition to benefit the students, in fact, was the topic for part of what they had listened to with the headphones. Remarkably, the students in the positive head movement group also responded significantly more positively in their opinion about increasing college tuition. Students in the negative head movement group thought the tuition should actually be lowered, and those in the control group remained neutral on the topic.

Not only did the body movement affect the rating of sound quality during the task in question, but it also affected the students' thoughts about the topic being discussed!

These findings open up a great possibility regarding the freedom we have to move toward greater happiness and flourishing. We have the capacity to influence the way we think and feel simply by shifting something in our bodies. It is very intentional that the mindfulness exercises begin with instructing you to move your body into a certain position. Sitting with your feet on the floor, sitting straight in a chair "with dignity," and lying down (as you will learn this week) all give you the best opportunity to take control of the way you use your mind and exercise your focus. We have centuries of examples of spiritual leaders and saints who taught how to pray using their bodies. Lying prostrate, kneeling, sitting with a certain posture, positioning our hands, and even making the sign of the cross are all intentional and meaningful parts of the way we position our minds and ultimately spirits to relate to God.

These findings relate to the philosophical principle of the unity of body and spirit. Ultimately we need to learn that our bodies are an integral manifestation of who we are as human beings. Our bodies are not something we *have*, but something we *are*. The popular sense is that the self is contained within the body, but the truth is that we *are* our bodies. It is more accurate to say that our bodies are contained within us than to say we are contained within our bodies.

Brother Ass

St. Francis of Assisi used to call his body "Brother Ass." He saw his body as a beast of burden that he had to beat into submission. This treatment was very closely connected to the way his father had treated him and what he learned about himself at an early age as a result of that treatment. St. Francis' dad beat him and locked him in the basement for disobeying his commands. At the end of his life, however, St. Francis apologized to this "brother" for treating it so harshly. He realized as he grew in perfection and holiness that his body was not something to be so suspicious of and violent toward. St. Francis changed the way he thought about himself over time, moving from the identity his dad had taught him to the way God—the "best of Fathers" (the title St. Francis often used to address God)—taught him about his identity as he grew.

Contrast this with St. Thérèse, whose father was extremely kind and generous with her. She called him her "king."[5] His fathering was much more closely aligned with the love of God, and consequently Thérèse learned more quickly who she truly was. It is no surprise, then, that St. Thérèse only briefly considered harsh corporal penance as a means to sanctity. She knew this was not the proper way to treat her body, and moreover she knew focusing on those penances would be more distraction than help. She still engaged in some corporal sacrifice such as fasting and enduring great discomfort at times, but all within a much better developed sense of the goodness of her bodily existence.

You might have a negative view of your body, or at least some part of it. Many people—especially in our culture, which is so obsessed with physical appearance—are embarrassed by certain physical imperfections, while others would much rather just forget about or ignore their bodies. When we let the assumption that something is bad about our bodies cause us to turn away and disregard them, we are disregarding ourselves. This is not to say there may not be some sickness or disease, or even a legitimate physical deformity, that we need to learn to accept. All sickness, whether psychological, spiritual, or physical, is a result of our original break from God. *Concupiscence* is the fancy word that summarizes all the ways in which our world, including us in it, has been affected by the turning away of humanity from God's plan. Still, though, despite how deformed or disordered anything can be in this world, the fact remains that the deepest identity of human existence is that we are created in God's image and are therefore good. This means that our bodies are therefore good, and to ignore or avoid them is to avoid something of God.

Cartesian Dualism: The Heresy We All Believe

What do you think of when you consider who "you" are? Do you feel like you are a being living *in* a body? Death is often considered to be a shedding of the body, and most people imagine the spirit leaving the body behind to ascend to heaven (maybe with a pit stop along the way). While there is some reality to the separation of body and spirit at death, it is an experience cloaked in mystery from a philosophical point of view, and not as simple as the popular mind-set understands it. This popular mind-set, inherited from the philosopher René Descartes, is called *dualism.* Dualism is the belief that your spirit and your body are two entirely separate things. Descartes' famous line, "I think; therefore I am," planted the seed to associate being human with the immaterial part of humanity (thinking) instead of the material, bodily part of humanity.

While it is true that there is a difference between the material and the immaterial part of who we are, that difference is not total. Human beings stand alone in all of creation as the only beings created as a union of the material and immaterial, body and spirit.

In the *Catechism of the Catholic Church* we read:

> The unity of soul and body is so profound that one has to consider the soul to be the "form" of the body: i.e., it is because of its spiritual soul that the body made of matter becomes a living, human body; spirit and matter, in man, are not two natures united, but rather their union forms a single nature. (*CCC*, 365)

Reintegration

We exist as a union of body and spirit, yet we act, to our detriment, as if we are separate. We ignore our bodies, moving through our day mostly unaware of what is happening in them. Mindfulness provides us with a practical reintegration of body and spirit by way of the mind. We spend time in the moment, aware of our bodies, and learn how to have a different relationship with our very selves.

God made our bodies with a tremendously complex system of sensory sensitivity. Researchers have only just begun to explore the real depths of the power of the human brain to understand the world around us. We don't need researchers to tell us what we are capable of in order to be capable of it, though. We can simply wake up to the experience that God created us to live out of.

A simple example of this is the stomach. You know what a "gut feeling" is, and you've probably experienced "butterflies in the stomach" before. The stomach is a central place of the body that experiences a great variety of consequences from mental events. Until recently, the true depth of this type of human experience was relatively unknown. Now, however, scientists are exploring the role that *neurons* play in the gut. There is a complex system of sensory neurons that communicate and exist between the stomach and the brain! The *enteric nervous system* is an exciting new area of research.

Again, we don't need researchers to tell us we have neurons in the stomach to know how important it is to pay attention to gut feelings. You do need to be aware of your body, though, in order to fully use the sensory system that God built into your being.

Adam, the young man mentioned at the beginning of this chapter, learned this principle after a few weeks of practicing mindfulness. He slowly began to understand that the ruminations of his mind were stimulating more physical responses in his body. He learned that he could simply turn away from the thoughts—mere "mental events" in his mind that he didn't have to give credit to—and turn back to the present moment. He knew deep down that God was in charge of it all, and his worrying wouldn't "add one cubit to his life." Now he was spending time each day learning how to put that faith into practice. Instead of trying to get ahead of every potential disaster in his mind to work out all the possible solutions, he was learning how to simply let each moment come and trust that God would provide him with everything he needed to take care of it. He gradually noticed that each moment, as it really was, was never as bad as he thought it could be. As problems came up at work, he realized that he was better able to handle each one of them with a calmer mind, and he could think "outside the box" more to solve those problems.

Radars and Amplifiers

Since we are an integration of body and spirit, each has a reciprocal effect on the other. When the body automatically experiences this type of feedback loop, without intentional awareness, it can turn into an *amplifier* of negative emotion. What starts off as a small thought of some concern turns into an anxiety felt in the body, and then the body's anxiety registers in the mind, leading to more anxious thoughts. Anxiety builds upon anxiety and the initial spark gets amplified.

When you wake up to this process, a new world of possibility opens up to you. God made your body with the capacity to feel physical consequences of the mental events occurring in your mind. In fact, he made your body capable of picking up on extremely subtle cues from the environment and other people, and even spiritual realities beyond the material world.

God designed the body to act like a *radar*, detecting movements within and without to help you make informed decisions about your life.

You may have heard the word *discernment* used in a spiritual context. It is built on awareness, and in fact years ago St. Ignatius developed a system of discernment known as the Spiritual Exercises, which is still very popular today. These exercises are founded on the ability to feel movements of consolation or desolation throughout the day. The Examen prayer, which is part of the Spiritual Exercises, is essentially an exercise in mindfulness, in which a person reviews moment by moment awareness experienced throughout the day. Awareness of the present moment is a prerequisite for the ability to practice the Ignatian exercise of discernment.

A typical practice of the Examen would look like this:

1. Take a few moments to sit in stillness and call to mind the presence of God. A few deep breaths help here. Ask him to be with you and help this prayer time bear fruit.
2. Review your day with a sense of gratitude. Find two or three things you are especially grateful for that happened today.
3. Scan the whole day, moment by moment, that you can remember, and see if any particular positive or negative emotions come to mind that you experienced.
4. Choose one of these emotions that you experienced and spend a few minutes with it. Consider what God might be saying to you through it. What can you learn about yourself or your relationship with him from this experience?
5. Make a commitment to some concrete action based on this realization.

As you can see, awareness of the movements inside you throughout your day is essential to this exercise. As you are scanning through your day and certain moments come to mind, it is important to evaluate them based on whether your body was acting as an amplifier or a radar. Why were you so upset at the guy who cut you off on the highway? Why did you back down from your coworker so quickly instead of sticking up for yourself? What was going on in your mind, in your body, and in your spirit? Awareness leads to self-awareness, and self-awareness makes growth possible.

The body is extremely sensitive to all kinds of emotional signals. When you learn how to diffuse the autopilot amplification of those signals, you consequently open the door to reading those signals as they really are, in each present moment. This is part of your intuition that God made you with to navigate the complexities of life. In order to access this powerful radar system, you must first learn how to pay attention to your body. This is how you can encounter the presence of God within you. He speaks to us in the quiet movements of our own hearts. There is no limit to which part or parts of the body can communicate reality to our minds.

Finding Peace

Remember that the human person *of God*, Jesus Christ, the model that all humanity was formed after, was made of the same stuff that you are. When you focus on your legs, you are focusing on something that is of God. Your stomach, even if you are conscious of having a few extra pounds there, is the *same kind of stomach that Jesus had*. He tasted with the same kind of mouth you have. The Son of God had normal bowel movements, vulnerabilities to getting cut or spraining an ankle, he cried when he felt sadness, and he felt the rush of blood to his face when he got angry. Your very body is sacred. You may have heard that you are a "temple of the Holy Spirit," but you are also more than that. You exist in the form that God himself would take if he were to enter into his created universe. He did this very thing! You can quickly turn the time you spend being aware of your body as it is into a prayer of gratitude, wonder, and awe at the creation of your own being.

Mindfulness is awareness of the present moment with acceptance and nonjudgment. The central being that is consistently in your awareness in each present moment is *you*. Therefore, mindfulness is a journey to find peace with yourself. Finding peace with your body is a significant step on that journey.

Mercy is at the heart of nonjudgmental awareness. A disposition of acceptance and nonjudgment toward yourself is a disposition like that of God, who sees you with the dignity he created you with, and looks with deep love and mercy at you. This gaze of love sees past the mistakes you make to the heart of who you *are*. It is far too easy to associate who we are with what we do. While it is true that our actions are important, there is a core of our identity that is deeper than what we do or don't do. This is the foundation of the gaze with which God looks at us. This is the gaze we need to learn how to look at ourselves with. Trustful surrender to God in the midst of any circumstance is possible only if we can experience deeply that God thinks we are good and worth his love. This sense needs to also inform the way we feel about ourselves.

This disposition will usher in the greatest peace you have ever experienced. As you chip away at the misconceptions and wounds you carry about your own body, or simply the disconnection you have from your body because of existing in a frantic state of putting out fires or moving from one rumination to another, you will grow in your interior peace. This peace nurtures a sense of goodwill that, when integrated with a mature spirituality and informed conscience, propels you forward along the path of conversion and human flourishing. You—an embodied spirit, perfect unity of body and spirit—are created for greatness. Your biggest obstacle to peace is between your ears, and the key to overcoming that obstacle is as close as your own body.

The exercise in this chapter teaches you how to open up awareness to all parts of your body. This exercise, called the Body Scan, is one of the most difficult to practice in the beginning, but it's one of the most rewarding in the end. It requires you to lie very still with yourself. It can also bring into your awareness deeply held insecurities you may have about your body, and it allows you to approach them with a new compassion, gentleness, and curiosity. It reverses the reasons mentioned previously for why people tend to ignore their bodies. This exercise helps to practically integrate the rift that has been created between body and spirit, along with healing those insecurities you might feel and helping you to develop your bodily radar. This seems like a pretty tall order. It is especially important to begin the Body Scan with a short prayer.

Since this exercise deals directly with our body, which many of us might have some issues with, the mind sometimes doesn't like to practice it. Resistance to spending time with your body can manifest in different ways. You might fall asleep, become easily distracted, or decide you simply don't have enough time for it. Remember that these are the ways the mind tries to maintain old habits, even if they are unhelpful. If you encounter these challenges during the body scan, allow yourself to acknowledge the difficulty, recognize the thoughts associated with it, then turn back to the body. Be gentle and compassionate with yourself. Be aware of yourself with curiosity, even if that means noticing the difficult thoughts that arise during the practice. Spending this time in mindfulness means you are choosing to spend time nourishing yourself, healing old wounds, reconnecting your faith to your life, and becoming the best version of yourself that you can be. It is worth it.

EXERCISE

Body Scan

Before you practice the Body Scan exercise and spend that time with your body, pray for the grace to have a disposition toward your own body befitting a creation of God. Imagine you are spending time at a museum admiring the work of a great artist. You are the greatest masterpiece created by the greatest Master in existence. You can use this time in open awareness of yourself with the awe proper to being in the presence of a masterpiece created by God.

During the Body Scan you might be frustrated by the lack of sensation in a particular part of your body. This is totally normal. When you've spent so much of your life unaware of your mind and even less aware of your body, it takes time to bring it into awareness. Imagine that you are narrating a wildlife documentary. As you progress through each part of the body in the Body Scan, it's as if you are an observer in the wild, simply waiting patiently for the object of your observation to appear. It is not your job to create a sensation. Many people feel that they need to move the body part to make a sensation arise. This is not the case. You only need to watch and be aware of whatever is there in your field of focus. For many people, various parts of the body will be silent at first. As you practice more, small flickers of sensation will gradually appear. You will sense more of your body as you become alive to your full self. As if meeting an old friend after many years apart, you will reencounter yourself much in the same way a child does. Childlike curiosity is the disposition you should seek to develop during this exercise. Allow yourself to be curious again, exploring the different parts of your body with open awareness and even delight at what you find.

This exercise is very good at illuminating all the ways the doing mode runs our lives. Don't be discouraged and give up when you come face-to-face with the doing mode. Instead, remember the things I've given you notice of here, and realize as they come up that they are supposed to appear. Remember that doing mode includes thoughts of judgment or criticism, thinking about how you want things to be instead of how they are, and trying to close that gap between A and B. Doing mode does not allow for thinking about the way you are thinking and instead turns on the autopilot. This is what happens when you are lost in thought and get carried away on a thought stream, avoiding feelings, thoughts, and sensations you don't like.

When these tendencies show up, you have a new opportunity to recognize it. You can think to yourself, "There it is, there's the doing mind! I know what to do with it. I will let it be." As your mind wanders to the past or the future, or you begin to feel restless, sleepy, agitated, bored, or avoidant, turn toward those experiences with awareness. Explore them with curiosity, then calmly and gently turn away from them and back to your body.

Pick a consistent time that generally works for you twice a day for a week. It is especially helpful to practice before times of prayer. You can also pray the novena included at the end of this book after one of your practices each day. This exercise in particular is best practiced while listening to the audio recording available at www.catholicmindfulness.com/audio.

- Begin by lying down, closing your eyes, and relaxing your body.
- Call to mind the presence of God, here with you now. Pray, "Ever-present God, here with me now, help me to be here with you."
- Bring your awareness to your body as a whole, noticing the sensations at the point of contact with whatever you are lying on.
- The intention of this practice is to spend time with each region of the body, cultivating awareness of what is already present, with acceptance and gentleness.
- Bring attention to the sensations of your breath. Spend a minute here, observing and resting in those sensations.
- Gather your attention and move it to your feet. Explore each part of each foot now, taking thirty seconds to do so.
- Letting go of the feet, move your attention to the ankles. Notice the sensations here.
- Now freely direct your awareness through the lower legs, to the knees, to the thighs. As you do this, allow your exhale to release the attention from that part of the body and

allow your inhale to move your attention to a new part of the body, beginning with the feet and moving to the ankles, then to the thighs.

- Bring the breath into each part of the body that you are focused on and then allow it to leave that part as you exhale.
- Remember, if you find your mind wandering or getting restless or bored, notice these feelings, acknowledge them, then gently escort your attention back to where you want it.
- Let go of any intention for your body. Allow it to be exactly as it is. Rest in the awareness of your body, part by part, moment by moment.

- Now, slowly and intentionally, on the in-breath move into the following parts of the body, then with the out breath move out of those parts of the body, spending one full breath in each part:
  - pelvis, hips (right, then left), back (lower first, then mid, upper, and entire back), lower abdomen, chest, hands and arms, shoulders and neck, head and face (lower jaw, chin, mouth, lips, nostrils, nose, cheeks, sides of your face, ears, eyes and eyelids, eyebrows, forehead, scalp, and entire head.

- Now breathe into your whole body with the in-breath. As you breathe out, notice the breath leaving the many parts of your whole body. Spend a minute here taking in the full sensation and awareness of your entire body.
- As you end, cultivate a sense of gratitude for your body and the gift of your life. Express gratitude to God for this body and the opportunity to spend time with it.

Habit Disrupter: Mindful Walk

Take a walk this week, by yourself, for at least fifteen minutes. Spend this time with your senses fully awake, turning away from the doing mode as it arises, gently escorting your attention continually back to your senses. Pay attention to everything around you as you walk, from the feeling and sound of your feet touching the ground to the sights, smells, and sounds coming from around you. Change your focus from things in your body to things close to your body, and then to things far from your body. Explore different ways of being present in this way while you walk.

CHAPTER THREE

Opening Ourselves to Freedom

He wants to be my peace so that nothing can distract me or draw me out of the invincible fortress of holy recollection. It is there that He will give me access to the Father and will keep me as still and as peaceful in His presence as if my soul were already in eternity.
—St. Elizabeth of the Trinity

Have you ever seen one of those braided tubes called Chinese finger traps? When you stick a finger in each end of the tube and then try to pull your fingers out, the tube narrows and grabs them even more tightly.

This is a good image for what happens when you try to solve problems in your life with the doing mind instead of beginning from a place of trusting entirely in God. As you wrestle through a situation trying to come up with a solution, your brain is firing away as if you are in danger, and this in turn narrows your sense of creativity. Grounded in faith that God is in control and everything will ultimately be well, we can explore solutions with an open and creative mind. Creativity is an essential element in problem solving, but it doesn't work very well when anxiety is increasing. This is also why people will often "sleep on it" when trying to figure out a problem or break through a writer's block. Letting the problem go for a time is like releasing your fingers from the constricting grasp of the finger trap. If you relax and stop the fight to free your fingers, the tube lets go and you can slip them out. When you let go of the idea that something is a "problem" that needs to be figured out, your brain relaxes the doing mode and you can open up to solutions you never thought possible.

The problem is that we have been trained from day one to solve problems, think critically, and work until we figure out the answer—or work harder. Even if we do have faith that God will make all things well, our society rewards this type of hyperproductivity and hyperachievement. At first glance, it seems that relaxing, sleeping on it, or letting go is just laziness. No matter how much we accomplish, many of us always feel that we haven't done enough.

That mind-set is the archnemesis of mindfulness. It is the reason why it can seem so hard sometimes to find the time to practice the exercises. It's simply too difficult to wrap your head around the notion that pausing your day to spend eight or ten minutes doing *nothing* can be a good thing. The real irony is that we end up wasting so much more time getting caught up in email, social media, news, or many other frivolous distractions. We never set out to waste that time; it just happens. To actually *plan* to do nothing "productive," though, is almost inconceivable.

The secret here is that practicing mindfulness will actually make your day *more* productive. I am not against productivity— quite the opposite, actually. I am trying to help you to be more productive. The research, along with the experience of countless business executives, entrepreneurs, and men and women trying to get more out of life, shows that spending time each day using mindfulness to reorient your mind changes positively how you relate to everything and everyone, making you more efficient and productive. God wants us to be more productive, and when we begin from a place of trusting him, we can be productive in a way that makes us the best version of ourselves.

We can also sense this in our spiritual lives. Sometimes we become frantic when we don't know what we are supposed to do. Discernment is a process that requires gentle peacefulness, and we need to slow down in order to hear the voice of God. In the Old Testament, Elijah met God in the "still, small voice" of a gentle breeze; God was not in the storms. We allow those storms to rage in our minds and hearts and we grow even more disquiet when we can't figure out where God is in the midst of it all. This is why St. Thérèse said she would "let Jesus sleep peacefully within her little boat"[6] no matter how bad the storm got or how much the waves crashed. She knew there was peace to be found in that storm, and she could simply quiet her soul knowing Jesus would take care of it if he needed to. This peace is necessary for you to be able to truly hear the voice of God. This interior quiet is the fruit of learning how to slow down and let your mind settle into the reality of the present moment instead of looking for God in the midst of the frantic thoughts and feelings.

In *Searching for and Maintaining Peace*, Fr. Jacques Philippe writes:

> Often we become agitated and disturbed by trying to resolve
> everything by ourselves, when it would be more efficacious
> to remain peacefully before the gaze of God and to allow Him
> to act and work in us with His wisdom and power, which are

infinitely superior to ours. . . . This doesn't mean we should be lazy or inactive. Trusting God is courageously and powerfully active. This is an invitation to act, even to a tiresome level at times, under the impulse of the Holy Spirit. This is not a spirit of disquietude, agitation, or excessive hurry, which is too often the case with us and the way we want to be active.[7]

Doing Mode and Creativity

One study[8] observed two groups of students completing a maze. One group had to move a hypothetical mouse through a maze to escape a hawk flying overhead that wanted to eat it. The other group had to move a mouse through the same maze to get to a piece of cheese at the end.

The maze was simple enough and there was no significant difference in the time it took the students to complete it. On the way out of the study room, however, the students were asked to complete a second, seemingly unrelated task. (College students are often getting tricked by psychologists.) This task measured the degree of creativity that was employed to finish it. Remarkably, the group of students who had solved the maze to save the mouse from impending death-by-hawk exhibited *50 percent less creativity* in the second task than the students who were simply moving the mouse to the cheese.

Spending as little as fifteen seconds solving the maze with the thought of a hawk eating a mouse on a piece of paper was enough to affect the group's brain chemistry and reduce their creative ability on a different task by 50 percent. Our brains are incredibly sensitive to the thought patterns we spend time with.

If a bear were chasing you in the woods, your brain would not waste resources on creative thinking. The sympathetic nervous response triggers automatic, autopilot actions. We conserve energy by being less creative when we are threatened. This is why it is so important to override the SNR when we are not actually being physically threatened. In many situations, it helps to have control of this response so that we can come up with creative solutions to solve our problems. Most military training involves desensitizing this stress response for exactly this reason. Even when a person's life is actually on the line, thinking creatively and outside the box usually proves to be a useful skill.

Perfectionism and a Sense of Responsibility

You may have a deep and possibly unconscious drive to prove something to the world (or maybe just yourself). This might have developed during childhood, adolescence, or your young adult years. Unless you were taught in word and deed that you are good enough just as you are, that you are valuable simply for existing and nothing further is expected of you for you to deserve positive attention, you may have picked up, at least to some degree, a sense of not being good enough. Bullying in the family or in the community can lead to a need to prove oneself as well. Sibling rivalry, parental issues or divorce, and many other dynamics can lead to these feelings.

Somewhere along the way you may have developed a script for perfectionism, one that says you are not doing enough, are not good enough, or don't work hard enough. This script perpetuates the doing mode, as it creates a near-constant problem to be solved. If this is true for you at some level, you are living in a perpetual state of escaping the hawk ready to swoop in on you at any moment. This mind-set reduces your creativity, closes off your perspective from the big picture, and prevents you from finding solutions to your actual, solvable problems with any outside-the-box thinking.

When we are young, this perfectionism script might be useful. We can be the best parents, best at business, best Christians. Our drive to escape the hawk keeps us going, and it can be easy to burn the candle at both ends. This is typical of college-age kids. Eventually, however, those thought patterns take a toll on the brain and that motivation gives way to fatigue. Negativity about oneself spirals into exhaustion, depression, chronic stress, anxiety, and a sense of defeat. Along the way on this spiral, creativity and playfulness disappear and you stop taking healthy risks.

Catholics are particularly good at maintaining this perfectionistic script. We look at Scripture such as "Be perfect as your Father in heaven is perfect" and think, "Oh great, what chance do I have?" We simply hijack religious ideas and conform them to our own disorder. This is not what God wants for us. In fact, perfectionism is almost the opposite of what that passage is all about, but we will come back to that later, in the section on mercy.

For now, you can take heart knowing that these are simply mental patterns that can be dissipated as soon *as you become aware of them*. Their power lies in going unnoticed, employed by the autopilot pretending to help you. When you shine the light of focus on them, you can stop the self-criticism and perfectionism dead in its tracks. You can see the way those thoughts drive you deeper into anxiety, which in turn moves you further away from an actual solution, and further away from any growth (spiritual or otherwise).

Even if we don't have a good sense of our real value or dignity, we still have that value and dignity. The beauty and the hope here is that who we are cannot be diminished by who we *think* we are. Rest assured that you are on a journey of discovery, and the final destination of this journey is to discover the person you've been all along. There is something about us that changes along the way, but the change is related more to our perceptions than to our core being.

Empathy and Tenderness

Another aspect of the doing mode is that it presents us with reality through a kind of filter. We don't see reality clearly as it is, but instead how we interpret it to be. This interpretation happens as a function of the autopilot. Once I was visiting some friends and heard their baby crying in the next room. The parents were out of the room for a moment, so I went to see what might be needed. I was surprised to find the older children watching a video online of cats making human sounds with their meows. My brain made a quick interpretation of the sound waves it was perceiving. It would take too long and too much of my cognitive capacity to listen to each sound wave as if I'd never heard sound before, and to explore every one as something new. The autopilot interpretations, therefore, create a kind of filter through which we receive reality. My association with the sound waves that came from a crying baby long ago had gone from my working memory to my autopilot, so those sound waves communicated to my mind in that moment that a baby was crying; I didn't think about it. Most of reality is experienced in this way—not as it really is but as it is interpreted through the filter of our autopilot mind.

That filter is forged by our own experience. Depending on what kind of experiences we have, our filter might include some level of problem solving. If I had a baby who was not sleeping through the night, and therefore not allowing me to sleep through the night, not only would I misinterpret the cat's meowing, but I also would have some level of an anxiety response associated with the sound.

Mindful awareness, therefore, allows you to see reality for what it is. It reduces the effect of the filter, as much as possible, and opens you up to a new experience of reality. This encounter becomes incredibly powerful when the object you are experiencing in your reality is *another person*. Here is one of my favorite applications of mindful awareness: **Nonjudgmental awareness of the present moment when the present moment includes another person, with his or her own thoughts and feelings, is foundational to truly encountering the other person as he or she really is.**

Mindful communication is the basis for the marital or relational therapy I provide. It also informs the way I try to relate to people in my own life (with ample room for growth). If you start to connect the dots here, you'll realize that not every conflict you have—unless it actually threatens your life—needs to activate your stress response.

I'll introduce you briefly here to the model of mindful communication that I employ in relationship therapy. It is grounded on the anthropology of St. John Paul II as expressed in *Love and Responsibility* and refers to a dynamic he calls "tenderness":

> The essence of tenderness is in the tendency to make one's own the feelings and mental states of another person. This tendency seeks outward expression: I feel the need to let the other "I" know that I take his feelings and his state of mind to heart, to make this other human being feel that I am sharing it all, that I am feeling what he feels. . . . Tenderness is the ability to feel

with and for the whole person, to feel even the most deeply hidden spiritual tremors, and always to have in mind the true good of that person. . . . Both in the woman and in the man tenderness creates a feeling of not being alone, a feeling that her or his whole life is equally the content of another and very dear person's life. This conviction very greatly facilitates and reinforces their sense of unity.[9]

Here you can read two ideas. One is a simple concept of empathy—to "make one's own the feelings and mental states of another." The second is also important for mindful communication: to let the other person know that you are empathizing. It is not good enough to simply feel what the other person feels; you have to let him or her know that you are feeling it if you really want to build that sense of unity.

Mindful awareness is necessary for the first part to even be possible. Empathy is that ability to make someone else's mental state your own. In order to do this, you need to be able to hear and see what the other person is saying, verbally and nonverbally, without it being filtered by your own interpretation.

A couple I was recently working with experienced this dynamic in the first session. Elizabeth explained that a fight had erupted after she'd commented that her husband, Bill, was "working a lot." He immediately grew defensive and started pointing out all the ways she was distracted from the family as well. While they sank deeper and deeper in the quicksand as they tried to fight their way out, they were totally missing the point of what had happened. By going back over the communication in my office, they traced the fight back to a simple misinterpretation. Even though it was an admittedly rare occurrence of affirmation, Elizabeth had actually been trying to express her appreciation for Bill's hard work. She was thinking that he deserved a break; she wanted to talk about a possible vacation.

They eventually got to the point where they could laugh about such ridiculous misinterpretations. Elizabeth recalled how one time Bill said to her, "You look nice today," and she felt hurt because she thought he was saying that she didn't look nice the day before. These kinds of misinterpretations happen all the time.

Mindful communication requires slowing down the process of communication. If we scrutinize an encounter between two people, as if looking through a microscope at the underlying principles that encounter is built on, we will find there are essentially two roles occurring at any given moment: *giver* and *receiver*. This dynamic is built into our very nature as human beings. It flows from the reality of being made in the image of God, "Male and female he created them" (Genesis 5:2), made to mirror his own Trinitarian existence. Every encounter between people is in some way a participation and reflection of the very being of God, who is an eternal relationship of giving and receiving between the Father and the Son. This is how we need to understand relationship in order to understand healthy communication. Starting from there, we can then break down what mindful communication looks like.

Since there are two modes of communication at the deepest level, we can actualize those roles practically while communicating. Specifically, each person needs to know what role he or she is playing at any given moment. At any one time, each person is either the giver or the receiver. Another way to say this is that one person is expressing while the other person is listening.

Most of us are really good at knowing when we are in the expressing role. As St. Teresa of Ávila said, "Many people are good at talking but bad at understanding." That's because most of us always want to be in the expressing role. We feel like our perspective or opinion is vital to the conversation, more so than the other person's, and so the motivation is to make sure that *our* side is understood.

Mindfulness is the key to unlocking thriving communication in your relationships because it teaches you how to lower your guard so that you can listen and understand. Having mindful awareness of the other person means hearing and understanding the thoughts and feelings of the person talking to you, without the filter of your own autopilot interpretations. As someone is talking to you about his or her perspective, especially in an emotionally charged conversation, you are certainly going to have all kinds of thoughts that cross your mind. You will be refuting the other perspective if it goes against yours, you will be figuring out where the holes are in the story or how the past events are being misremembered, or you will simply be thinking about how you are so misunderstood. This can happen in a boardroom or a bedroom. It happens anywhere there are two people with different perspectives. Those thoughts are like clouds floating past in the sky, and your practice as someone in the listening role should be to turn back to the present experience of the other person's thoughts and feelings that are being expressed. Just as you learn how to redirect your focus from critical thoughts about yourself when you are trying to pay attention to your breath, you can turn your focus away from critical thoughts of the person speaking and back to his or her actual thoughts and feelings.

Some people object at this point of the process and say, "How will I remember what I was thinking if I simply turn away from my thoughts to pay attention to the other person?" First of all, you can hear in this statement just how unhealthy our mind-set can be. You really can only pay attention to one or the other. If you choose to pay attention to your own thoughts and feelings, you won't be paying attention to the other person. Second, this is where trust comes in. Trust yourself and your ability to know what is important to you. The doing mode will only block you from how you really think and feel. The autopilot defensive interpretation will narrow your focus and restrict your memory. It will also bias your perspective, and you will be *less* in touch with how you really feel. When you learn how to be mindfully aware of the other person, regardless of your own thoughts and feelings, you enter into the being mode with the full capacity of your mind. The disposition of kindness and compassion that you are cultivating toward yourself in your practice is then directed toward another person. This helps you realize more deeply what is actually important to you.

Next, when the other person has fully expressed his or her perspective (and you've reflected back with your words the notion that you've taken it in and felt it as your own), you switch roles. At that point you get to sit in the expressing seat, and go back to your own thoughts and feelings that you previously turned away from. If you really can't remember what they were, they probably weren't that important. If they are important, you now have a partner who is willing to listen to you and understand your perspective as if it were his or her own.

That willingness might seem difficult to achieve. It certainly helps if the person you are communicating with is aware of this dynamic that you are trying to create. It's even more helpful if he or she is practicing mindfulness and reading this as well. Interestingly, this is the type of communication that is employed by expert hostage negotiators in the most difficult situations. The other person doesn't even have to know you are trying to communicate this way in order for it to work, even in a situation as tense as a hostage negotiation! Mindful awareness makes this kind of communication possible.

Building Mindfulness into Your Day

So far you have been learning more about how your mind works. You've been introduced to exercises that help you to stabilize your mind and focus your attention where you want it to go. Hopefully by now you are waking up to routines in a way you've never experienced before and learning new things about yourself. You are learning that your thoughts are not you, and you can change the way you relate to them.

You may have also experienced the frustration or sense of failure I mentioned in the beginning. At this point I have had students in the past who have said, "I understand I'm not supposed to be clearing the mind, and I get that certain thoughts might always pop up, but I still don't see how I'm supposed to *control* them!" This is a normal thought, but it is still a misconception. Our goal is not to empty the mind, and it is not to control the mind. It certainly might be a nice side effect that we notice a decrease in the number or strength of anxious or depressive thoughts, but that is not our goal in the moment for our exercises. As you are practicing, your goal is simply to wake up and become aware of things as they are. These exercises are meant to train your focus muscle so that you can pay attention to those thoughts that are crossing your mind and be in a state of curious awareness, simply watching them as they float by. Mindfulness is nonjudgmental awareness because judgment is an added thought that we pin to the first thought that springs up spontaneously. If we simply observe the spontaneous thought without adding another thought to it, it eventually floats right by.

EXERCISES

Sacramental Pause

This next exercise will take you a bit deeper into the integration of formal mindful practice with the normal living out of your day. You've already practiced mindful awareness of routine behaviors, but this chapter introduces you to a new exercise you can use throughout the day. It is something I call a Sacramental Pause. Fr. Jean-Pierre de Caussade refers to what he calls the Sacrament of the Present Moment. A sacrament is an encounter with God. Fr. Caussade teaches us that because God is an eternal moment, when we place ourselves mentally in the present moment, we are placing ourselves in the presence of God. In a very real way, we are encountering God by mentally focusing on the present moment.

The Sacramental Pause is one of the recorded exercises you can practice this week by listening to the audio available at www. catholicmindfulness.com/audio, or you can simply look at the steps and practice it in the quiet of your mind. I recommend setting a time twice a day to do so. Many people have told me the Sacramental Pause is the most powerful thing they learn from this book. Students practice it long after they've gone through formal mindfulness training, and you will see it has the power to radically affect your day. It is essentially a way of quickly reconnecting with God throughout the busyness of the day, so you can imagine how powerful that might be.

This is a simple way to incorporate a quick formal practice into the normal flow of your day. It is also an incredibly effective way to diffuse difficult and distracting emotion as it occurs. Therefore, it is a kind of emergency exercise you can employ as needed. It is good to punctuate your day with this exercise at least twice at regular intervals, and then to use it whenever you need to. This exercise will become a powerful ally for your mental health as well as for your spiritual well-being.

Pick a consistent time twice a day that generally works for you. It is especially helpful to practice before times of prayer. You can also pray the novena at the end of this book after one of your practices each day.

- This can be practiced sitting up or lying down.
- Begin in prayer: "Ever-present God, here with me now, help me to be here with you."
- Bring your awareness to what is going on inside you right here and now, and acknowledge it.
  - What thoughts are going through your mind? Acknowledge these thoughts as mental events.
  - What emotions are here? Turn toward any uncomfortable feelings and acknowledge them. Don't make them go away; allow them to be here, just as they are.
  - What body sensations are here right now? Acknowledge these physical sensations as they are; don't try to change them in any way.

- Now bring your awareness specifically to the physical sensation of your breathing. Feel the expansion of the breath as it comes in and the contraction as it goes out. Follow this movement of breath for a few moments. Use each breath to anchor yourself to this present moment. If your mind wanders, simply escort it back to the breath.
- Open your field of awareness from the breathing to the physical sensation of your body as a whole. Feel your whole body, as if your whole body is breathing. Imagine that the breath can move into and around any sensations of pain, discomfort, or tension. Take a moment to stay with each part, moving only after these sensations have stopped pulling for your attention.
- Bring your attention back to your awareness of sitting, being aware of your body moment by moment.
- Allow this exercise to last as many or as few minutes as you like.
- As the exercise ends, spend a moment thanking God for this time, for his presence here with you, and for your capacity to be aware of all that is right now.

There is a general flow to the sacramental pause that we will be adding to in the following chapters. Start with prayer, open your awareness to any thoughts, emotions, or physical sensations, then narrow your focus to the physical sensation of your breath alone, and finally expand the focus to the physical sensations of your whole body.

Mindful Movement
The other exercise this chapter introduces is called Mindful

Movement. Many times people find a moving body easier to pay attention to than a static body. Lying down or sitting can be more difficult, and so this exercise provides you with a new kind of laboratory to explore the way your mind works. It also gives you the opportunity to begin playing with the experience of staying mindfully aware of discomfort. The movement is specifically designed as a series of stretches. You will be guided to stretch parts of your body to their limits, which will trigger sensations and thoughts you wouldn't otherwise have. These new sensations will help you exercise even more your ability to stay in the present moment amid a whirlwind of different kinds of thoughts. It will be natural to feel a bit awkward as you begin these exercises, but as always, use those thoughts as new material to be aware of, then turn back to your practice.

I want to repeat that the point of this exercise is not to produce painful sensations. Be very attentive to your own needs, and if you have any physical difficulties, do not practice this exercise without first speaking with a physician. You will learn how to explore different uncomfortable sensations and experience the limits of your body. You need to move slowly, checking in frequently with your intentions and thoughts if you begin to feel pain. It is OK to slow down, pause, or simply stop the exercise if you need to.

One of the points of this exercise is to learn how you have different levels of discomfort and that you don't have to anticipate them all the same way. You can think of it like wading into the ocean. There are certain levels of discomfort that we will call shallow water, and then you go deeper and deeper until you can no longer touch the bottom. In the deep water, discomfort becomes pain that disturbs your ability to focus so much that you get swept away in rumination. For this exercise, you want to explore where the shallow water of discomfort ends before turning into the deep water of pain that sweeps you away. Don't go into the deep water—stay where it is shallow and you can stand firmly, in control of your focus. Once you find that point of discomfort, you will learn you can stay there, exploring it, without worrying that you will drown simply from being in the water at any depth.

The Mindful Movement exercise is followed here by the Mindfulness of Body and Breath exercise from chapter one. Try to practice this combination of exercises at least five days in the next week. Notice if there are any differences in your practice of the chapter one exercise from when you first practiced it.

- Call to mind the presence of God, glorifying him with your body. Repeat to yourself, "Ever-present God, here with me now, help me be here with you."
- Stand with bare feet or in socks, with your feet hip width apart, parallel to each other. Keep your back straight but not stiff.
- Feel your head balanced, shoulders relaxed, with hands by your sides.
- Be gentle with yourself during these stretches. Allow the body to inform you of your limits as you move.
- Cultivate awareness of the body; even the smallest movement is important to notice.
- Begin by noticing the contact your feet have with the floor.
- Taking an in-breath, slowly and mindfully raise your arms out to your sides until they are parallel with the floor. Hold this position for a moment. Exhale.

- On the next in-breath, continue to raise your arms slowly and mindfully until your hands are above your head, with the palms turned in toward each other.
- Stretch upward for a few breaths, maintaining this position to experience the shallow water of discomfort, but staying within your limits.
- Slowly, very slowly, on an out breath, begin to lower your arms back down. Breath by breath, really tune in to the changing sensations as your arms move. Allow your hands to rest, arms hanging from your shoulders.
- Focus on the sensations of your entire body and the after-effects of the movement on your body.
- Now stretch your right arm up, as if trying to grab something that is just out of reach. Pay attention to the sensations of your body (from your fingers to your breath) as you stretch. It is OK if your heel is raised.
- As you lower your heel and your arm, follow your fingers with your eyes, taking in the colors and shapes around you.
- Focus on the sensations of the aftereffects of this movement on your body, also paying attention to your breath as it moves in and out of your body.
- Repeat this stretch with your left arm.
- Note where the edges of your limits are, becoming aware and then letting go of the tendency to push beyond them.
- On your next out breath, put your hands on your hips, allowing your head and shoulders to lean over to the left very slowly and mindfully, with your hips moving a little to the right. Your body will form a curve. Breathe in and out as you hold this position for about thirty seconds. Pay attention to

even the smallest movements your body is making during this stretch, focusing on the sensations that are present.

- On an in-breath, return to standing upright. Remain here for a moment. On an out breath, slowly bend in the opposite direction. Take a moment to be aware of the sensations that are present. Then on an in-breath, slowly return to standing upright. Allow your arms to gently fall to your sides and rest. Stand like this for just a moment in order to take in the after-effects of this stretch on your body.

- Now raise your shoulders to your ears as far as they will go. Begin to roll your shoulders from this upward position to the back, then down and forward. Continue this rolling motion, paying attention to all the sensations that arise from it. Notice your muscles, your skin, the clothes on your body shifting. Bring your focus to these points. Let your breath determine the speed, breathing in for half the movement and out for the second half.

- Change directions, rolling your shoulders forward.

- On your next out breath, allow your body to return to stillness, motionless and relaxed.

- Take a moment to become aware of any and all sensations in your body from the aftereffects of these stretches. Bring your awareness to your breath coming in and out of your body.

- Now practice the Mindfulness of Body and Breath exercise as described in chapter one.

- As you end this exercise, cultivate a sense of gratitude by thanking God for your body and for this time you were able to spend with him here, in this present moment.

Habit Disrupter: Digital vs. Analog

The Habit Disrupter this week has to do with technology. I believe one of the reasons mindfulness has become so popular—and so necessary—with our culture is the massive proliferation of digital technology. I am not anti-technology by any means—I employ it to deliver the Catholic mindfulness course to thousands of people and use it in many ways in my own life—but I do think we've let it get out of control. I don't think anyone would argue that point, but I also haven't found many people who are willing to do something about it.

As you learn more about the way your brain and mind work, you will understand more clearly why digital technology can be so unhealthy. Hold your phone for a minute. It's probably not far from you right now; if it is, touch whatever screen is nearby.

Touch the digital device near you as if you were practicing the raisin exercise. Look at it, feel the contours and texture, notice the way light plays off it. Rub it on your cheek; tap it and notice the sounds it makes. If you spend even five minutes doing this, you will experience this device in a way you've never experienced it before. Even if you've owned something like it for ten years, you've probably never spent even five minutes *actually with it*. This is why digital technology can be so unhealthy.

Every time you use this device, or watch TV, you practice anti-mindfulness. Imagine how many hours you have spent practicing anti-mindfulness exercises, in which your mind is *not aware* of what is actually present in the moment. In this time and space, it is a phone, or TV, or whatever, but your mind is focused on the news, or social media, or shopping, or whatever it is that you are looking at.

Analog technology is the direct reproduction of data based on what is in the present moment. Think of a record player. The needle moves over grooves on the plastic disc. That is translated into electrical impulses, which produce sound waves, and your ear hears them. Digital music turns those sound waves into electronic representations of ones and zeros. They can be reproduced anywhere in the world, at any time, totally separate from time and place. This analogy isn't perfect, but it makes sense to some degree to show how much we are separating ourselves from the present moment with all the time we spend in the digital world.

Pick one day this week when you will take a technology holiday. Purposefully set aside this day and decide not to check email, look at the computer at all, or even watch TV. Spend just one day without electronics. This might take some planning. Obviously if you have to use technology for work then you can set limits for it and use it as little as possible. (You most likely don't have to check email every fifteen minutes.) If you use the Internet for recipes or directions, try to get those things ahead of time so you aren't dependent on it during your technology holiday. Set an auto-responder on your email or just forget about it for the day. Participate in this exercise as much as you reasonably can given your specific circumstances. If there is a day when it might be easier to follow through, do it on that day (Saturday or Sunday, for instance).

CHAPTER FOUR

Telling Ourselves Stories

When thy mind dwells upon anything,
Thou art ceasing to cast thyself upon the All.
For, in order to pass from the all to the All, Thou hast to deny
thyself wholly in all.
—St. John of the Cross

John was on the way to the hospital.

He was worried about what people might say.

He never had all the answers the patients wanted from him.

It wasn't the janitor's job to answer their questions.

As you read those sentences, the picture in your head probably went through different phases. Each line added a new piece of information that you tried to fit into the picture you had already painted, and you repainted it as needed. Maybe you first pictured a guy named John but weren't sure why he was going to the hospital. When you heard about his concern, you might have thought he was a patient who'd received bad news. Then you read he was going to be asked questions, and so maybe you thought he was a doctor. After the last line, you realized he was a janitor.

This is the way our brains work. One function of your auto-pilot is to fill in the gaps based on the information you have, to make up for the information you don't have. You make the best guess possible about those gaps based on your own experience and memories that come from the pieces of information you are given.

There are differences between the ways different people interpret various pieces of information based on their own experience. Two people can have radically different interpretations of the same event. Most of life is experienced not directly as it is, but how you interpret it. How you see things is really more dependent on who *you* are, and not how the world actually is.

The ABC Model

This process, as described in a psychotherapy approach called cognitive behavioral therapy (CBT), is called the "ABC" model of perception. In this model, A represents an event as it really exists in the world, B is the interpretation our mind makes about the event, and C is how we respond to our interpretation.

Most people assume that when we react to something, we are reacting to the thing itself. In actuality, though, we are responding to an imperceptible and immediate interpretation that we make about the data we are receiving, not the data itself. Earlier I gave the example of hearing what sounded like a baby crying. My mind and emotions responded as if there was a baby crying, yet it was really a cat meowing. The real-world event was the sound waves created by the cat. Those sound waves traveled through my ears and caused a reaction in my brain to give the impression of sound, and then my mind interpreted that sound and labeled it "baby crying." My interpretation happened to be wrong in that scenario, which is helpful to illuminate the different parts of the perception process. Later in this chapter you will learn an exercise called Mindfulness of Thoughts and Sounds, which will use the reality of sound waves to help you develop an even deeper focus on the present moment.

Imagine that you are out at some public place, such as the grocery store or a restaurant. You see someone you know pass by, and you wave, but she does not wave back. What story does your mind tell you about the fact that she didn't wave at you? You may think the person saw you but ignored you for some reason. Maybe she's upset with you or doesn't have time to stop and chat. You might reason that maybe she didn't see you, and then you question whether it was obvious that you were waving. These different interpretations can lead to different kinds of emotional responses. If you feel insecure, you might interpret the situation in a way that devalues you ("I'm not worth speaking to"). If you believe people are often looking for a conflict, you might think the person is mad ("What is she upset about now?"). Different people have different kinds of thoughts, but they are all examples of interpretations. The reality of the other person not waving back (A in the ABC model) does not cause the consequent emotion (C), but the interpretation (B) does. We are responding to our interpretations of the world, not to the world itself.

The existence of this B level of interpretation is almost always imperceptible, because it happens so fast that it becomes woven in with our experience of reality itself (A). We combine B with A, so we think we are reacting to things as they are. This B layer of interpretation becomes like a rumor, though, that grows, and it can morph into a kind of propaganda that we fall prey to in our life. Think about the idea you have about yourself that you simply don't have enough time in your day. This belief can take many forms. You can look at the reality of the time in the present moment and be triggered to a number of different interpretations. You might simply think at times, "If only I had more time," or "I'll never feel like I am ahead of the game." You might think life could be better if you could just get enough items crossed off your to-do list. Not having enough time is a common belief that almost everyone suffers from.

Time

When I was in college, I didn't think I had enough time to get all my studying, extracurricular activities, and part-time work done. When I went to grad school, I looked back at college and realized how much free time I had then. In grad school, I felt like I was drowning in classes, papers, practicum, dissertation work, and an actual job. Every year of school grew more difficult and I looked at first-year students with envy. When I got married and moved to New York City to start my practice, I thought, "Now, *this* is busy!" My wife became pregnant right away, and I had six months left of her supporting us financially to get my business going enough so that I could take over the financial responsibility of our new little family. Day and night I spent studying about business, making contacts with priests and other people in the Church, and trying to grow the CatholicPsych Institute. I was going full throttle, and if I ever had a minute to remember my days of grad school, I could easily get lost in the fantasy of how glorious all my free time then was.

Then we had our first baby, Elijah. As most people experience with their firstborn, our lives were drastically changed by our son's arrival. Never before had I experienced such joy, cocreating a human person with my wife and God, and never before had I experienced such . . . sleeplessness. Adding a third person to the picture whom I was responsible for stretched me to a whole new level of understanding time. With less sleep, more responsibilities, and a brand-new growing business, not to mention a still-young marriage that also required time and effort, I looked back at our life in our first apartment before Elijah and realized I actually did have a lot of time then.

How does this make sense? At every stage I felt like I was doing as much as I could, and with each new responsibility I realized that I'd been wrong. *My sense of time was based on an interpretation of reality, not reality itself.*

Three more children, a second business, and developing my individual practice into a group practice with six therapists has finally taught me that *time is a matter of the mind.* Through daily practice of mindfulness, I have finally crossed a certain kind of threshold and often feel like I have as much free time now as I did in the carefree days of my childhood. It was actually my children who really helped solidify this for me. Pope Francis has said a number of times to parents, "Don't be afraid to waste time with your children." This really convicted me. Early on I saw the way I was prioritizing the means to take care of my family (work) over the time I actually spent with my family. Without really knowing how it would work out, I jumped into "wasting" time by doing nothing with my children. They are all really young (four and under at this point), so there isn't the possibility yet of pretending I'm spending time with them while also doing something productive. ("Come on, son, let's clean this grill together.") Letting time with my children be a kind of practice in mindfulness has helped me open up productive and efficient ways of seeing the rest of my day.

Learning how to stay aware of the present moment has given me back my time, even as the number of things I do increases. This is a radically different experience from any I've ever had in my life, and it seems to be a radically different experience from most people's. How often do you respond, "Busy," when someone asks you how you are doing? Because of how much I have going on, others often approach me with, "I know you must be really busy, but . . ." and I just smile to myself. It feels wonderful to be able to say, "Not busy at all—how can I help?" *Busy* is really just a code word for *mismanaged*. The autopilot mind is not well equipped to create efficiency in the big picture of your life. When you don't practice mindful awareness, you are giving the authority of your life over to this part of your mind that is meant to operate only in emergency situations. Don't be surprised, then, when the way you manage your time makes you feel like you're on the brink of an emergency.

You will learn through this journey that the more mindfully aware you become throughout your day, the more you will find pockets of time—whether it's five minutes or an hour—to nurture yourself. It doesn't matter what kind of responsibilities you have in your life. Your mind-set, or belief system, creates a filter of interpretation through which you perceive reality. If you think you don't have enough time, you won't. If you think you do have enough time, you will. Practicing mindfulness can be difficult at first because you begin from a place where you are still operating under the interpretation that you don't have enough time. The more you practice, the more you will realize you don't have enough time *not* to practice it. This is a learning process, though, and it takes time to develop the experience.

A Deeper Look

This is exactly why you must learn how to be patient with yourself. It is an exercise in itself to pay attention to the thoughts you have about the way you are experiencing this book. Have you gotten frustrated with yourself? Have you found yourself getting frustrated with me? Have you criticized yourself for not trying hard enough? Have you felt exasperated that you haven't put in enough time for the practices? Maybe you are still young enough to be riding that wave of perfectionistic motivation and you meticulously practice every exercise, but then you find "evidence" that you didn't do them correctly. Or maybe, like many people, you have experienced very positive results from mindfulness so far, but you are starting to see how other people in your life might need it as well.

Everyone has moments of judgment, and the way you judge can be very interesting to observe. You can become like a scientist, carefully observing the intricacies of thought that arise while you are learning about mindfulness. You can be like a nature observer, studying the movements of some animal in the wild. Your thoughts are that animal, and the mind-scape is the environment in which you observe its behavior. Whatever you do, separate yourself from those thoughts, realizing that you are not those thoughts and you can stand back from them to observe them as they are, in the present moment. You can use even those negative thoughts about your way of practicing mindfulness as a way to grow in awareness of the present moment.

Self-Criticism

Self-criticism in general can be a particularly deep and difficult interpretation to grab hold of with mindful awareness.

Interpretations in the mind can be true, somewhat true, mostly false, or entirely false. Taking them at face value and believing them wholeheartedly simply because the thought occurred doesn't seem to make much sense. Mindlessly following your thoughts from one to the next as if they are true simply because they happened doesn't make much sense either. Especially when you're feeling stressed, the inner voice of criticism speaks louder than any other voice. You might try to hear another voice of compassion, but because of the stress, you won't believe it. You also might try to shake yourself out of it, telling yourself to stop "beating yourself up." As you engage in the battle with those thoughts, though, and end up switching from one perspective to another, an overarching sense of negativity only grows stronger. The battle itself can further lower your mood.

If left to themselves, these thoughts then seek further evidence of their own truthfulness. You might begin to think of all the other times you were similarly deserving of self-criticism. Your brain presents evidence as if prosecuting a court case. Another part of you may step in to argue against the case, but the case itself becomes a "problem" to solve, which activates your doing mode, setting you further down the path of mindless unawareness. Trying to solve a problem narrows your perspective and drives you from criticism to dislike to despair.

Fighting against negativity with different forms of "positive thinking" is not the best approach. It makes much more sense to simply step out of the courtroom altogether. You can step out of the thought stream, watching the negative thoughts float by as if you are sitting on a riverbank watching leaves float by on the water. Even if you are sitting next to rapids, with turbulent water crashing over rocks, you can still sit safely on the side.

Here is a list of thoughts to flesh out this idea. These are examples of interpretations that might float through your mind when you are feeling stressed, exhausted, or otherwise unhappy:

- I can't allow myself to fail.
- I can't relax without checking everything off my list.
- It's all up to me.
- I'll never be able to relax!
- I can't let everyone down.
- I have to be the strong one.
- Everyone is counting on me.
- I'm the only one who can do this.
- I can't stand this anymore.
- I don't want to waste time.
- I wish I were somewhere else.
- Why don't they just do it?
- Why am I not enjoying this anymore?
- What's wrong with me?
- I can't give up.
- Something has to change.
- There must be something wrong with me.
- Everything will fall apart without me.
- Why can't it stop?
- How am I going to deal with this forever?

It is so hard to separate ourselves from these thoughts when we are stressed because they feel true. It feels like the thought is who we *are*. The truth is, though, these thoughts are mental events that occur at a specific moment in time, and we can turn toward them instead of being in them. Moreover, these thoughts are actually symptoms of stress, and you can read them the way you would read a thermometer when you have a fever. The more thoughts like this, the more stress you have. The more you believe those thoughts, the stronger the stress is that you are feeling and the faster it spirals. "I'm going to mess this up" turns into "No one else will be able to do it." "They depend on me; I'm going to let people down" becomes "I can't take this anymore," and "I just want to disappear."

Mindfulness practice will help you to create a space between you and these thoughts. In that space—a few split seconds, maybe—you will have the freedom to choose how you will relate to those thoughts. This is how mindfulness helps you become more fully the man or woman God created you to be. In that space, you will have greater access to your *gift of free will* that God created you with. Instead of mindlessly believing those interpretations your mind holds on to, you can stop to observe and evaluate them. You can decide, with practice, that they are simply manifestations of the stress you are feeling and they don't deserve your attention.

Autopilot Glue

When the doing mind perceives a thought, it begins the process of habituated associations. Just like when your brain hears a sound and automatically associates a label with it, when you first think a thought you associate other thoughts with it. Think of those associated labels or thoughts as glued to the first sound or thought, creating a chain. Each link of the chain is glued to the next because the mind is in autopilot, or doing mode. When you turn your focus toward your thoughts, you will notice that you have fewer of them. This is because you are overriding the doing mode, entering into the being mode and giving your autopilot a break. When you look at the first thought that pops up in your mind, you dissolve the glue, which means fewer thoughts will be added to it. There certainly can be some additional thoughts that follow along, but the more you practice, the more you will notice thoughts becoming more like sounds to you. New ones will continually appear in the mind-scape, but they will not be the result of habituated associations that create chains of thoughts.

Often when I am sitting somewhere, anywhere from the car to church, my mind will wander. Sometimes it can be progressing through this thought chain for an entire ride to work, or through an entire homily. Recently I passed by a work crew setting up a carnival. I started thinking about taking my kids to the carnival on the weekend and wondered if they were old enough to enjoy it yet. Then I started thinking about developmental stages of children, which led me to thinking about my children as teenagers. I thought about some of the patients I have and the stories I hear about what teenagers are exposed to and what a tremendous responsibility we have as parents. Then I thought that I sounded like my parents must have sounded when they were raising me and I started thinking about my aging.

This all occurred in about two minutes. Thinking like this is a normal daily experience for everyone. We don't notice what's happening in our minds, and we don't realize that on some level, the survival instinct God created us with is actually operating in those moments. Right around the point where my ruminations turned toward wondering if I had a big enough life insurance policy to take care of my family should anything happen to me, I "snapped out it," or "came to my senses." I realized I was in a thought stream, the autopilot had taken over, and I was not being mindful. I reminded myself that God is in charge, he alone knows what will happen in my future, and he loves me and will take care of whatever I need. I could then examine the thoughts for what they were, simple mental events passing through my mind. Turning toward them as such stopped their progression. The glue dissipated.

Each time your awareness drifts away from the thoughts as they are, or your being mind slips back into doing mind, new chains are formed. Each new stimulating thought is a new temptation to follow it with habituated associations. Patience with yourself is necessary. This is bound to happen over and over again, as your mind will randomly and continually produce new thoughts.

Isn't That a Judgment?

I want to pause here to briefly explore an idea that will come up often in the course of this material and in life. Something we encounter often, but at times have difficulty really processing, is the existence of *paradox*, or an apparent contradiction that when explored deeply turns out to be true. In psychology we have a term, *cognitive dissonance*, to describe the mental discomfort that comes from holding two seemingly contradictory ideas in our minds at the same time. We have a mental drive to quickly judge one of the ideas as false in order to relieve this discomfort. Sometimes, of course, one of the ideas we are holding is false, and so it is good to discern what to reject. In the case of a paradox, however, there is a way in which both ideas can be true. We have an opportunity to grow in wisdom through the process of trying to make sense of how that can be. Many errors in science, philosophy, and religion occur as the result of too quickly writing off a contradictory idea as false. For example, most of the divisions in the history of

Christianity are based on a rejection of some idea about Christ. Is he both God *and* man? Are we both saved *and* responsible for our actions? Does God love us with both mercy *and* justice? Is God both three *and* one? The answer is yes, all are true. Figuring out how requires sitting with the initial discomfort of not knowing how it could be true, and deepening our understanding of the different facets of the problem until it makes sense.

You are learning that mindfulness practice is supposed to be nonjudgmental, noncritical, and based on the idea that you are safe and don't need to "solve a problem." Yet throughout this book, I am often giving examples of the problems people have in their lives and how mindfulness is going to solve them. You might feel that you are trying to solve problems in your life by employing this "problemless" practice, or convincing yourself that there really are no problems. That can be frustrating because you know there really are some problems, and the whole point of picking up this book might have been to solve them. So what gives? This is not a question you will find an adequate answer to in the secular teaching of mindfulness, because it requires a perspective of the human person that includes the spirit as distinct from but integrated with the body.

If we revisit the reality of the union of the body and the spirit for a moment, we can move toward an understanding of this paradox. St. John Paul II wrote:

Created in the image of God, man is both a corporeal and spiritual being. Bound to the external world, he also transcends it. Besides being a bodily creature, as a spirit he is a person. This truth about man is an object of our faith, as is the biblical truth about his being constituted in the "image and likeness" of God.[10]

"Bound to the external world, he also transcends it." We exist with the co-occurrence of two principles within us: spiritual and bodily. This is the reality that can relieve the discomfort of our mindfulness paradox. Freedom exists within the spiritual principle of our existence. It is a faculty of our spiritual principle, not our bodily one. This is good news for people who suffer from disease or disorder based in the body (which also includes the brain and the great effect our bodies can have on our emotions and the thoughts in our mind). As long as we are conscious, we have access to a spiritual dimension of human freedom.

This freedom is active when we think about the goals we want to live for. Patients who suffer from addiction may not have much freedom in the deepest throes of their addiction—the moment when they actually take the drug or the drink—but they have freedom before that. They can choose to get themselves into treatment, to attend meetings, or to avoid people, places, and things that lead to the point of no freedom. The "external world" that a person is bound to in this case includes a brain that is so affected by biochemicals that the reasoning part of it can be turned off at times. The part that transcends the external world, the spiritual principle of the addict, is the part that can choose not to place himself in that situation in which his prefrontal cortex is inoperable. Another way to understand choice is to see it as a kind of judgment. We can make transcendent judgments about how to direct our lives.

In many ways, our thoughts and bodies are determined by the physical, material world. Your thoughts are affected by the chemicals in your brain. You read already that simply moving your head in a certain direction can affect the opinion you have about something. Every second, there are thousands of physical interactions happening at the microscopic level that dictate a lot of what we experience.

Along with the moment-by-moment effect of these determining interactions there is a transcendent capacity to know truth in an abstract way and make choices to move in a certain direction with our actions.

We can call these two levels *transcendent* and *immediate*. These words will be helpful to answer our question about mindfulness practice. In order to pick up this book, you made a transcendent choice to learn something new. You may have decided there is something to be gained by reading this book—there was something you wanted to add to or change about your life. At the same time, the thing you decided to read about teaches you to let go in the immediate moment of what needs to change. Holding on to those thoughts through autopilot ruminations and the doing mind works against your goals. In a way, letting go of what needs to change will help you change what needs to change.

This is a very subtle and almost imperceptible distinction. In each moment, you may be aware of your transcendent judgment to let go of immediate judgment. As you continue to practice, keep a small "light" of focus turned on, waiting to sense what that transcendent awareness feels like.

Ironically, it is by letting go of immediate judgment that we greatly develop our ability to make healthy transcendent judgments. The resources we need to perceive any given situation in the context of our whole lives are available to us only when we have a sense of safety and security—when our fight-or-flight, doing mind is turned off. Intuition, creativity, and wise perception are all increased by relaxing our need to judge each thought passing through our minds. Then we can plot the course we want our lives to take and intentionally set out to be the best versions of ourselves.

Begin Again

The more you practice and the further you advance in this book, the more you will experience your own wandering mind. That is because when you first start, you are less aware of when your mind wanders. As you develop your awareness, the wandering mind becomes clearer to you. Instead of being lost in a thought stream for five or ten minutes at a time, you more quickly come to your senses and return to the exercise. If you can refocus every minute, it makes sense that a ten-minute exercise will be filled with ten experiences of refocusing instead of just one or two. Even though it feels like failure, it really is not. The more you practice, the more you will "fail."

This is very similar to the spiritual life. The more you develop your conscience and self-knowledge, the more you realize your faults and want to grow out of them. Fr. Jacques Philippe wrote in *Searching for and Maintaining Peace*, "The sign of spiritual progress is not so much never falling as it is being able to lift oneself up quickly after one falls." This sounds very similar to Williams and Penman, who wrote in *Mindfulness*, "The experienced mindfulness practitioner is not someone whose mind does not wander, but one who gets very used to beginning again." We must learn how to begin again. We must become like beginners who are comfortable with the fact that we are beginners.

To become like a beginner is similar to being like a child. In a lot of ways mindfulness is about cultivating a childlike disposition toward ourselves and the world around us. Children are typically carefree. They have an innate sense that their world is protected and they are cared for. Their needs are met without them knowing how or why. This allows children to remain playful and curious about their world. They are receptive to reality as it is around them and are naturally more aware of the present moment. This is the disposition we are called to have, even as adults. We are all called to be like children, as Jesus instructed. We are told to trust in the Father, who loves us and takes care of all things.

Beginning again, over and over, may start to feel a bit repetitive. If you feel bored at times because of how repetitious the exercises are, take heart and realize that they are meant to be so. This is one way that mindfulness can be a bit difficult, but it is incredibly rewarding. If you think about it, you are living your life with many autopilot behaviors, which are by nature repetitive. The ways you think, feel, judge, perceive, and act are in many ways repetitive. By learning how to shine the light of focus on those functions, you will stop repeating the way you relate to your life. It is through the repetitious exercises of mindfulness that you become aware of the way repetition has been hiding in your mind all along. It is through the habit of mindfulness that you learn how to escape the habits you didn't realize you had.

EXERCISE

Mindfulness of Thoughts and Sounds

In this chapter's exercise, you will be moving from developing a general awareness of what mindfulness is and how to apply it practically in your life to a deeper awareness of the ways your body and mind signal warnings to you. First you will need to become more comfortable with the uncomfortable signals that your body may be giving you. You learned last week how to sit in the shallow waters of discomfort physically. For the next step, you will learn more clearly how thoughts are harmless things that you can sit with as well, as if they are also shallow water discomforts. In order to do that, you will practice an exercise called Mindfulness of Thoughts and Sounds.

Your ears are receivers that are constantly picking up sound waves around you. Our world is immersed in sound. If you've ever been in a house that's lost power, you've noticed immediately the absence of the sounds that you've learned to tune out. The sound waves created by the hum of appliances and the air blowing through the vents have always been there, but you've hardly heard them. Stepping out into the wilderness is another way to experience what silence actually feels like. The sound of a leaf rustling underfoot seems amplified against the backdrop of real silence.

In this exercise, you will learn more about your own thoughts by way of analogy to sounds. Hearing and thinking are similar in a lot of ways. Sounds and thoughts both arise seemingly out of nowhere. They seem random and are not things we can ultimately control. They can trigger strong emotions and cause our thoughts to run wild. These similarities will help you use your awareness of sounds to become more comfortable and tuned in to your awareness of thoughts.

You can think of your ear like a microphone. As an instrument, a microphone simply receives sound waves and transmits them to a receiver. The microphone itself doesn't modify or add anything to the sound wave. Our ears do the same thing. They simply receive and then transmit sound waves to the brain. With hearing, though, there is almost always a second step of judgment that occurs, in which a label is applied to the sound experience. You immediately categorize the sound you are hearing, thinking the words *cat* or *baby* or *running water*. Similarly, the flicker of a thought will also trigger a series of other associated thoughts. Each thought then becomes a trigger for the next. What started off as a single event, comparable to hearing a sound, turns into a spiral of associated thoughts that can drag you into negative places. Most thoughts, even if they start off positive, can eventually become associated with unsettling ones in the doing mode.

You will learn how to relate to your thoughts the same way you can relate to sounds. You can simply let your brain be the receiver of the mental stimuli that your mind is transmitting to it, just like your brain can be the receiver of the external stimuli your ear is transmitting to it. When one sound triggers the neural network starting with your ear, it is a momentary event. A new sound can then occur as an entirely different and unrelated event, and your ear hears it for what it is, forgetting about the previous sound. It just receives what is there in each passing moment. You can let yourself be aware of your thoughts in the same way. You can experience the thought for what it is while keeping your awareness open, just like when you are hearing, moving from one sound to another. You can also think of your thoughts like the sounds coming from a TV or computer: You don't need to believe everything you hear. It is simply noise that you might have to listen to if it is on, but you don't need to give credit to it as true.

These thoughts, like sounds, come out of nowhere, and they can be very disturbing or unsettling. You never know when one will appear that strikes a deep chord of experience, triggers a deeper sense of fear or insecurity, and therefore shuttles you back into a thought stream or rumination. Each time this happens, you have simply to pick up where you left off once you are aware of what happened. With calm, patient gentleness, gather your focus back up and turn it toward the exercise at hand.

Pick a consistent time twice a day that generally works for you. It is especially helpful to practice before times of prayer. You can pray the novena at the end of this book after one of your practices each day.

- To prepare to enter into this exercise, first practice the Mindfulness of Body and Breath exercise from chapter one, beginning as always by calling to mind the presence of God.
- Now focus your attention on hearing. Open your awareness to sounds as they arise, near or far, in front, behind, at the sides, above, and below.
- Notice any tendency to label sounds as they come or to judge whether you want them to be here. Notice how easily distraction can come and how easily sounds can create a story.
- As you notice this, bring your attention back to the sounds in and of themselves. Allow them just to be sounds, to be just as they are. Stay with these sounds for a moment now.
- Imagine hearing these sounds for the very first time, as if each one were new to you. Explore them with curiosity, observing what is here. (Cultivate a sense of wonder, not taking for granted the gift of hearing.)
- Hear the pitch, the loudness, the rhythm, the intricate sounds within sounds, and the quiet space between sounds.
- Strain your ears, fine-tuning your sense of hearing to pick

up on all the intricacies of sound around you, the difference
between sound and silence, and the various textures and colors of the sound.

- Now let these sounds fade into the back of your awareness,
  and bring your attention to your thoughts. What is here?
  (worries, to-do list, thoughts about the past or the future, etc.)
- There is no need to control your thoughts in any way. Let
  them come and go on their own, just as you did with the
  sounds.
- When the thoughts or images arise in your mind, try to see
  them like clouds passing in the sky. Your mind is like the
  sky and your thoughts are like the clouds. Sometimes these
  clouds are small, sometimes large, sometimes dark, sometimes light. But the sky remains as it is, unaffected by them.
- Use this image to see and experience your thoughts as mental events that arise in your mind. They may stay around for
  a while and then move on, just like the clouds in the sky.
- Emotions may arise while you do this. See if you can be open
  to everything, no matter what it is.
- Rest now for a moment in this open awareness.
- Your mind may wander, getting drawn into different stories
  by your thinking. Use your breath as an anchor, focusing on
  it to stabilize you in the present moment, should this happen.
- Focus your attention again on the coming and going of your
  thoughts and feelings. Stay here for a moment.
- Now bring your focus to your breathing. Expand this focus
  to also take into account the awareness of any thoughts
  or feelings that pass through. With practice, you can learn
  how to pay attention to both at once, feeling the physical

sensations of your breathing and sensing the thoughts or feelings that pass through.

- Remember that your breath is always available to help bring you back to the present moment. This practice allows you to cultivate and access a deep stillness and peace no matter where you are or what is happening.

- As this exercise ends, bring your awareness to the presence of God, here with you now. Allow your mind to tune in to the loving warmth in which he embraces you. Let yourself feel gratitude for his presence in your life.

In addition, continue practicing the Sacramental Pause (chapter three) twice a day, or anytime you feel yourself getting caught up in ruminations.

Habit Disrupter: Trip to the Movies

For this chapter's habit disrupter, take a trip to the movies. Go alone or ask someone to go with you, and only pick the time to go. Instead of researching what movies are out and planning on the time based on what is playing, just choose a time. Then go to the theater, and choose a movie once you get there.

By locking ourselves into certain beliefs such as, "I can only go to the movies if I know the movie I am going to see," we miss out on enjoyable experiences that nourish us. Sometimes the best movie is the one you had no idea you were going to watch. Additionally, the act of watching a movie can sometimes be ruined by the process of choosing one (like trying to pick a streaming movie at home).

Pay attention to the thoughts and feelings you have about this exercise, but then turn away from them and jump right in.

CHAPTER FIVE

Running Away

When I see that the burden is beyond my strength, I do not consider or analyze it or probe into it, but I run like a child to the Heart of Jesus and say only one word to Him: "You can do all things." And then I keep silent, because I know that Jesus Himself will intervene in the matter, and as for me, instead of tormenting myself, I use that time to love Him.

—St. Faustina[11]

To help make this real, I want to share with you a tragedy I recently experienced. My mom passed away in January 2015. She was far too young and had been far too healthy, but was diagnosed with an aggressive form of cancer and died within a few months.

I was in the middle of teaching a Catholic mindfulness course when she became really sick and was admitted for the last time to the hospital. As much of a fighter as my mom was, the last few weeks were especially terrible as the cancer started to win. In between work I was spending most of my time at Sloan Kettering, and doing my best to stay focused on whatever was before me. Switching back and forth between taking care of my responsibilities and spending time with my mom in the last weeks of her life was one of the most difficult things I've ever had to do.

There is a novena we pray as a part of the course I teach (the one included at the end of the book), and it includes the Father speaking words to us about staying at peace when we see people around us getting sick. I put the novena together months before my mom was ever sick, but I stared at the words, sometimes with shock and disbelief, as I read them to the class. I'd had no idea how necessary those words would be for me when I wrote them, but I clung to them and received immeasurable consolation from the providence of God. My family and I held on to hope, treatment after treatment, even as the reality of death grew closer. We didn't want to, but we had to learn how to accept the inevitable, and to accept each other's way of coping together as a family.

It was through this horrific ordeal that I knew God was with me more than ever before, and I also knew that he was asking me to do more with my course. Through every treatment, every moment of disappointment when the treatment didn't work, every vital sign that looked more and more bleak, there was one place to go where the sadness was washed away by a reality far greater than you or I could believe was possible in such moments. It was in each present moment that I knew God was with me. Each moment invited me to turn my mind toward the his presence, the ineffable reality of love that created the universe and brings everything to its final destiny. It was in the immensity of God's love that I saw, in each moment that I needed it most, the smallness of life on earth as we know it, and the immeasurable greatness of eternal life. It was only when I had the humility to turn away from the way my limited mind understood things that I had the freedom to turn toward things as they really were. It was in those moments when I turned from the ruminations and toward the pain with acceptance that my eyes met God's. There in that stillness, when the frantic rush to make sense of things I didn't understand paused, I heard him say, "Let me take care of it. Everything is going to be OK." I wrote this book to share with you that peace.

Acceptance

My efforts to make sense of things that didn't make sense to me were ways of avoiding the pain and avoiding the reality of not being in control. It doesn't have to be the death of a loved one that causes us to employ these tactics. It could simply be job-related stress, illness, financial hardship, relational conflict, or a host of other experiences that we'd rather not go through. When faced with difficulties, we naturally try to avoid them. We can endlessly ask why or let our lives pass by while our minds are stuck in problem-solving mode. We can bury our feelings under other feelings such as anger or perfectionism, or we can simply distract ourselves with a thousand other realities that seem more important to us in each moment. No matter how long we've lived and how long these methods have failed to actually make the bad things in life go away, we still run away from difficulties.

Even if running seems to work at first, eventually we break down. Sooner or later we realize that our coping methods create difficulties worse than the original difficulty itself, or that the difficulty is so strong that we can no longer ignore it. It is at this point—and sometimes it is the worst difficulties in life that bring us clearly to this point—that we can learn how to form a different kind of relationship with difficulty.

This new relationship is one of acceptance. *Acceptance* is a loaded term, and we need to break down exactly what it means. The root of the word comes from the Latin word *captum*, which means "taken." To accept means to take something in, which is an active process; it requires a choice. This is very different from a passive resignation to stop fighting things that are bound to happen, to give up and surrender in defeat. It is also very different from a kind of passivity that leads to apathy. To accept one's suffering is not the same as not caring. It is extremely different for me to say that I accept the fact that my mom died of cancer than to say I don't care. Sometimes the presence of peace in a person's life can be so difficult to understand that the only feasible conclusion might be that the person didn't really care in the first place. I think the more extreme the difficulty, the easier it becomes to see the difference between acceptance and apathy.

This chapter may bring up painful realities from your life. It is OK to slow down and be gentle with yourself, no matter how you feel. Whatever feelings arise, greet them with compassion and listen to the voice deep within you. If instead of plowing ahead you need to take a step back, revisit some of the earlier exercises, and then come back to this chapter later, it is OK to do so. No one is keeping track of what you've done or not done; there are no grades here. I encourage you not to give up, though, and to come back to it. Choosing to accept life as it unfolds is one of the most important things you can do. Every other exercise and experience mentioned previously has led up to this point. You have learned how the mind works, we've explored why your mind does what it does, and now you are going to begin the process of changing the deepest layers of your beliefs about your very self.

Two Roads Diverged

The work I do has exposed me to some of the most horrific realities of human suffering imaginable. The pain of losing children, suffering severe trauma, or living through torture is tough to describe. I've also seen how difficult it can be for others to process situations that might not seem so bad to others. It has taught me that it doesn't really matter specifically what people suffer—everyone suffers.

People's experience of suffering is very much relative to their own lives. At the end of the day, every person has a choice to make about which path to take when confronted with suffering: avoidance or acceptance. Every difficulty you encounter comes with this choice.

If you listen closely, you can hear the words of Christ as he invites you down the path of acceptance. "Do not be worried about the things of your life." "Trust me." "Be like children." This path looks scary, but it is actually the only path of peace. The path of avoidance, on the other hand, is wrought with constant anxiety, worry, and insecurity. Even in the best moments of ignoring, distracting from, or covering over suffering, this path is accompanied by the realization that your alleviation of suffering is only temporary, because it hangs on your own efforts and does not ultimately bring real peace.

The path of acceptance is the one you walk with peace, but peace does not mean the alleviation of suffering. Peace is that deep, interior stillness that tells you that no matter what kind of catastrophe might be happening in your life or in the world, everything is going to be OK. It is the sense that there is a meaning to all of this, even if you can't understand it. It is the sense that someone bigger than you is in charge, that the weight of the world does not rest on your shoulders, and that it is OK to break down and not be "strong enough" (no one is strong enough). The reality is that no matter how much money you make, how great a family you have or come from, how successful you've been in life, or how many people count on you to take care of things, you still know deep down that it could all fall apart at any moment. The path of acceptance is the realization that it is OK to be in need, like a child, which resonates with the deep sense that you really are just a child. You actually can't stop tragedy from happening, you can't block suffering, and you are not strong enough to protect yourself from every possible danger. This is the sense of being a child, and the only way to peace is to know it is OK to be a child because you have a Father who loves you and takes care of you.

As you step out onto the path of acceptance, become aware of the temptation to avoid suffering. In our exercises, this means tuning in to the inclination to avoid, ignore, suppress, or distract yourself from any unsettling thoughts, sensations, and emotions. As you practice the new exercise this week, pay careful attention to the way your body and mind react to the oncoming experience. The next step along the path of acceptance is to meet those experiences with a new sense of welcoming. If they are unpleasant, you can greet them as you would an unsavory houseguest whom you've decided to welcome hospitably into your home. Instead of locking the door and turning out the lights, pretending nobody's home and hoping the person will go away, you put on coffee, change the sheets in the guest bedroom, and open the door with a smile.

Acceptance Is Abandonment

There is always beauty in the deep layers of life. That doesn't mean that evil is beautiful, but evil is never the deepest layer. Even when the situation is evil on the surface, there is always a deeper layer where the immortal truths of existence form the foundation of our lives. Jesus is always victorious—that is the deepest truth. God has already conquered death, and we no longer need to live in fear. It is this foundation that we can stand on so that we may have peace no matter what happens. It is what Christ assured us of; we can believe in it by faith. God has made all things well.

In the midst of our deepest pain, we want to be in control. We want to be able to ask why and have an answer that is acceptable to us. We want to rely on our own strength of mind. Yet this is not the way of faith, and it is not the path to holiness. It is not being as children who trust in a Father who loves us. Fr. Caussade writes:

> The divine action, although of infinite power, can only take full possession of the soul insofar as it is void of all confidence in its own action; for this confidence, being founded on a false idea of its own capacity, excludes the divine action. This is the obstacle most likely to arrest it, being in the soul itself; for, as regards obstacles that are exterior, God can change them if He so pleases into means for making progress. *That which God wills for this present moment is best*, and all else must be regarded by the soul as being nothing at all.[12]

Fr. Caussade is saying that when we don't submit ourselves to God, giving up our own understanding of things, we don't allow God to work fully in our souls. Our interiority—in other words, the choices we make with our wills whether to accept that God is lovingly in control even in the midst of suffering, believing that somehow his providential love is still true even when we can't see or understand it—is given to us alone to steward. That is the place of our greatest choice and dignity as human persons. That is where our transcendent selves, our spirits, can choose our own path either toward or away from holiness in any given circumstance. Fr. Caussade says in this passage that the interior life is the place where God *won't* force us to change the obstacle into a means for growth. It is up to us to make that choice; God does not take it from us. It is only when we make this choice to abandon ourselves to him that we can truly find peace. This is my experience in losing my mom to cancer, and it is the example of countless others who have suffered unimaginable tragedy and yet persevere with interior peace.

Mindful Birthing

While death is one difficult experience to accept, birth can come with its own set of difficulties. One recent example of mindfulness making a big difference for people is in the area of childbirth. The labor and delivery process can certainly be incredibly painful. However, as is taught in systems such as Mindful Birthing[13] and Hypnobirthing,[14] a lot of the discomfort comes from the tension created by two opposing muscle systems in the body. The muscles in the uterus that contract to help a baby move out of a woman's body are opposite the muscles that tense up during stress. These two muscle systems oppose each other the way your biceps and triceps do, but they also overlap each other in the abdominal area. For this reason, learning how to calm the sympathetic nervous response during labor significantly helps reduce the discomfort felt from two muscle systems working against each other. When the body's fight-or-flight response is calmed, the contractions in the uterus are given full freedom to move the baby out for delivery.

Remember that the foundation of Catholic mindfulness is trust in God. He is the Father who provides everything for us that we will ever need. Remember also that in the Garden of Eden, the serpent tempted Adam and Eve to doubt the goodness of the Father. Do you remember what one of the consequences of this original sin was? "To the woman he said, 'I will greatly multiply your pain in childbearing; in pain you shall bring forth children. . .'" (Genesis 3:16).

If the multiplication of pain in childbirth is the consequence of Eve's sin, and her sin was fundamentally doubting the goodness of the Father, then is it too much of a stretch to consider that restoring our trust in the Father by letting go of worry and living peacefully in the present moment can help reduce the consequence of original sin? Christ died for our sins to restore humanity to a relationship with the Father. Certainly we will continually be fighting against the effect of sin within us, but we also must hope in the power of the cross. Whatever can be made of these theological points, the fact is that practicing mindfulness in the process of childbearing is significantly reducing the experience of pain for many women around the world.

This reality hit home for my wife, Barbra, and me recently as we were expecting to bring our fourth child into the world. My wife (who gave me permission to tell this story) has experienced certain traumas in her life and has battled anxiety for many years. She began practicing mindfulness to help with the labor of our third child, and it significantly reduced her discomfort. This fourth time, however, mindfulness practice so greatly reduced her anxiety response that she didn't realize how far into labor she truly was. Because she was only feeling discomfort, not the pain commonly associated with childbirth, she assumed this was still the prodromal or "false" labor that she had experienced in the past. Barbra was unknowingly almost all the way through the labor process by the time she felt the need to leave for the hospital. We called our friend Annie to stay with our other children so that we could leave, and by the time she arrived at our house, it was time to push the baby. Despite my initial protest, I quickly saw the reality of what was happening. With a few quick contractions Barbra delivered our daughter, with Annie's help, in the bathtub! While I have a firm appreciation for the advancements in medical technology that make us all safer and healthier, I now also have a greater appreciation for the satisfaction and peace that comes from experiencing such miracles of life in the comfort of one's own home (though for anyone hoping to go this route, I definitely recommend a properly planned home birth over stumbling into an unassisted birth like we did!).

Exploring Difficulty

The exercise for this chapter will introduce you to a way of sitting with unsettling situations in your mind. Everything we have covered up to this point has been a preparation for this, and so you will use the skills you have developed thus far. Before practicing the exercise, you will begin with the Body and Breath exercise along with the Thoughts and Sounds exercise. You have been gradually building your stamina for more prolonged practice, so this exercise will be a bit longer than previous ones. It is very important, however, that you prepare for the Exploring Difficulty exercise by doing the other two. If you don't have twenty minutes to yourself, simply end with the first two exercises, but don't try to practice Exploring Difficulty on its own.

This exercise can be seen in two parts. You will intentionally call to mind a difficult situation, but then turn your attention immediately to your body. When the difficult situation comes to mind, you will be tempted to stay with your thoughts and start to work through the situation, either mulling it over or trying to solve it, fantasizing about how it could have gone differently or how it might go. Your thoughts might also lead you to consider other difficulties in your life, and the thought stream could pull you into a spiral in which you think poorly of yourself or criticize or judge yourself harshly. These are all actions of the doing mind, and we want to cultivate an awareness of these tendencies. Then, instead of letting them happen blindly or on autopilot, you will turn your attention away from the difficult situation in your mind and observe the way your body is reacting to it.

There are two reasons why we turn to the body immediately after calling these difficulties to mind. The body gives you a space between your thoughts and their pull that whispers to you, "Danger!" You can turn from your thoughts to your body, and in this turning, you have a moment to realize there is a difference between thoughts and reality. When you try to stay in your thoughts and observe them, it is far easier to get lost in the negativity and continue down the spiral of autopilot problem solving. This is because your focus is positioned in your mind, where your thoughts are. Your sensing abilities directly involve your thoughts. If you are thinking about your thoughts, it is much easier to get lost in them. If you are thinking about your body, it is easier to maintain your awareness, your intentional focus, and your freedom of choice in the moment when you choose what you are doing with your mind. "Thinking" indicates simply the basic awareness of focus, not the "thinking about" that is indicative of a thought stream. Both happen in the mind, and there is a subtle difference that is important to notice. Turning from the difficulty in your mind to the physical sensations in your body will help you develop an understanding of that difference. It will help you develop thoughtless awareness.

The second advantage to turning toward the body is that you will more clearly experience the constant changing of your body state. One lie of the doing mind is that the negativity you're experiencing will never go away. This lie is part of the stickiness of that glue that holds together the associated thoughts in the thought stream. You feel that if you don't figure it out, you are doomed. When you turn your attention to your physical sensations, you realize that those sensations are almost always fluctuating. As bad as a feeling might be, when you turn your focus toward it, you will see it has many different parts, and those parts shift and change. States of mind and the kinds of thoughts you have also fluctuate in much the same way. By experiencing this reality first in your body, you will start to dissolve the stickiness of the glue that can hold together your ruminations. You can learn that negativity doesn't always stick around, and you don't have to feel like you are doomed.

When you practice this exercise, you can use a difficult situation that is not that difficult. You don't have to call to mind the worst thing that has ever happened to you. You can simply consider an uncomfortable situation, a time when you weren't at your best or when something didn't quite go your way. The goal here is to create an experience to exercise your focus with. At this point in your journey, you may find it is a little more difficult to stay with the experience you are invited to focus on in the exercise. Calling to mind a difficult situation pulls a little harder at your tendency to want to problem-solve, analyze, or become lost in sadness or anger over it. As these inclinations arise, moment by moment, continue to gently and peacefully turn your attention back to your body.

As you focus on your body, tune in to any area where you feel physical discomfort. Your heart might be racing, or your shoulders might be tense. Perhaps you realize you've clenched your fist, or maybe your jaw. You may feel something in your stomach, or some kind of pain in your back. Your tapping foot might come to mind, or even clenched toes. Sometimes you might not seem to be able to find any physical sensation, but keep your awareness open. Imagine your mind's focus is like a radar, simply scanning the body to see where and when some blip appears. Move to wherever there is a stronger sensation. You'll spend a few minutes on each sensation, and then, just as you did with the Body and Breath exercise, you'll "breathe into" that area.

It's OK to Feel This

At the deepest level, you want to enter into a slightly more uncomfortable state while maintaining the sense that it is OK to be here. Saying to yourself that it is OK to be here is like keeping the doing mode switch off. If it's not OK, there's a problem that needs to be solved. This is why you practiced the Mindful Movement exercise in chapter three—you have learned how to sit in the shallow water of discomfort. You've learned that it's OK to feel discomfort. Emotional pain might be very uncomfortable, but it is all in the realm of the shallow water of discomfort. (Remember the deep water of discomfort was unhealthy physical pain.) The types of physical discomfort that accompany emotional pain are typically not life-threatening or physically dangerous. In fact, even in extreme cases of emotionally triggered physical discomfort, such as a panic attack, treatment begins with teaching that a person can't die from such discomfort. As uncomfortable as it is, it is OK to have a panic attack. This is the first step in treatment because believing otherwise only more strongly activates the sympathetic nervous system, which increases the level of anxiety and produces more panic attacks.

While the physical discomfort might be OK to feel, you may be triggered too much mentally by the thoughts you are calling to mind. If you find that you are unable to maintain focus on your body and the thoughts are too strong to use for this exercise, it is good to take a break. You can practice the first two exercises and stop without doing Exploring Difficulty, or try to call to mind a less difficult situation. Think of the analogy of sitting on the riverbank while you watch the stream flow by. This is the position you want to be in as you watch what happens in your body as a result of the uncomfortable situation you've called to mind. Sometimes after a heavy storm, the stream turns into a raging river, and it even overflows the riverbank. The place you could normally sit peacefully is now underwater. If you try to sit there, you'll be washed away. If you find that you are being carried into the thought stream because of the situation you've called to mind, the pull of that situation is too strong at this point and you should let it be for now. After a few more days or weeks of practice, you will find that the waters have receded, and you can come back to those thoughts and maintain open awareness of the present moment through your intentional focus with much greater control.

It is also helpful to continue the practice with less difficult thoughts. Remember, the point is simply to find something that triggers a physical reaction and then become aware of those bodily reactions. Awareness is the first step to dissolving the glue that allows the autopilot thought streams to take over. It is the manual override switch that turns off the doing mind. In this exercise you are strengthening your awareness. You are learning here to have a radically different relationship to the difficulties that arise in your mind. You are learning that it is OK to think and feel certain things, that you don't need the autopilot problem solver activated at the slightest hint of difficulty, and in fact, you will be able to solve your problems much more effectively when it's not.

When you know it is OK to feel this way, you can then become like the explorer who is curious about uncharted territory. You are the wildlife observer open to anything that comes across your field of view. You are the playful child, wide-eyed and excited to explore an expansive new world. This awareness will certainly take in painful realities, but it will also keep you open to seeing the deep beauty that lies inherently in all of life.

EXERCISES

Exploring Difficulty

Pick a consistent time once per day that generally works for you. It is very important that when you practice the Exploring Difficulty exercise this first week, you precede it with the Body and Breath and the Thoughts and Sounds exercises. This means that if you don't have enough time for all three exercises, only practice the first two and do not attempt Exploring Difficulty on its own. Try to make time at least four days during the next week to practice all three together.

- Call to mind the presence of God: "Ever-present God, here with me now, help me to be here with you."

- Practice the Body and Breath exercise from chapter one.
- Follow with the Thoughts and Sounds exercise from chapter four.
- Give yourself a few moments here, open to awareness, allowing your mind to move between what is present in the thoughts, the sounds, your breath, and the sensations in your body. Notice anything and everything that is here now.
- Up until now, you have been instructed to gently escort your mind back to the breath when it wanders to some problem solving or distraction. For this exercise, you will explore a new possibility. Instead of turning away from a thought or feeling, I invite you to allow this thought or feeling to remain in your mind.
- Let this difficulty that appears in your mind sit for a moment. And if no difficulty naturally arises, go ahead and call some difficult thought or feeling to mind—something recently or from long ago, not the most difficult, just something uncomfortable.
- Allow this to rest in your mind. Stay here and slowly explore it for a moment.
- Then move your attention from this thought to your body. What sensations has it stirred within your body? Take a moment and be aware of any physical sensations the difficulty is bringing with it.
- Intentionally bring your focus to the region of your body in which these sensations are strongest. Breathe into that part of the body on the in-breath and out from that part of the body on the out breath. You are not trying to change these sensations; you are merely exploring what is here. Notice how the intensity changes from moment to moment.

- Say to yourself, "It is OK to feel this. It is OK to be open to this."
- Give the sensations your full attention, breathing with them, letting them be.
- If something else appears in your awareness, let your focus turn to that in your body. Other parts of the body may come into focus. Remember, you don't have to like the feelings in your body. It is natural to not want them around. But here, you are safe to allow them to exist, to be open to them just as they are.
- On each out breath, soften and open to the sensations, wherever they are in your body, letting go of the tendency to tense and brace against them.
- Stay with your awareness of the bodily sensations. Be aware of how you are relating to them, and breathe with them. Let them be just as they are.
- Should this difficulty soften and fade, move on to a new one.
- When you are ready, return your focus to your breath moving in and out of your body.
- As this exercise comes to an end, turn your mind back to the presence of God. Thank him for this moment, this breath, this mind, and his promise to take care of you no matter what you are going through.

Sacramental Pause

Continue to practice this twice per day. Additionally, you can use it anytime you realize you are starting to ruminate or some worry is sweeping your focus away.

Advanced version: This week add these points to your Sacramental Pause practice.

- Describe, acknowledge, and identify thoughts, emotions, and physical feelings during part one.
- Add the phrases "breathing in" and "breathing out" to focus even more on breath during part two.
- Expand attention to specifically include discomfort, tension, or resistance in the body during part three.

Habit Disrupter: Same Seat

Think of an activity you do every day but with some variability. This could be a place you sit while watching TV, the order of things you do to get ready in the morning, or the manner in which you execute any number of things during the day or before bed. Pick a certain way you will do this activity differently and stick to doing it that way every day this week.

CHAPTER SIX

Living in Love

*If I did not simply live from one moment to the next, it would
be impossible for me to keep my patience. I can see only the
present, I forget the past and I take good care not to think about
the future. We get discouraged and feel despair because we
brood about the past and the future. It is such folly to pass one's
time fretting, instead of resting quietly on the heart of Jesus.*
—St. Thérèse of Lisieux

Shame

Think of a moment in your life that you replay over and over
again. This moment is something that comes back to you often
throughout your life. It might be a mistake you made or something you could have avoided. There are probably several such
moments, but typically they are not positive events. An extreme
example of this kind of replaying is experienced by people who
suffer from post-traumatic stress disorder, or PTSD. With PTSD,
there can be a chronic reexperiencing of a traumatic moment.
The mind replays over and over again a certain event, as if
searching for something. Everyone has this mental capacity, and
experiences it to some extent. The more pain or discomfort that
is felt in the moment, the more the memory can "stick."

It is very easy for the mind to slip into a thought stream that
starts with the spark of a memory but then develops into thoughts

such as, "What could I have done differently?" or "If only that hadn't happened." These thoughts can swirl into "I'm not as good as I could be," "I was dealt a bad hand," and "I wish I was better than I am." This happens to everyone, not just those who are diagnosed with PTSD. Memories lead to ruminations about the negative feelings associated with them, and then they morph into ruminations about oneself. This is the nature of the doing mind on autopilot. We often live as though our mistakes, shortcomings, and sins are unforgivable—and certainly unforgettable. But how does God think about those same faults and failings?

St. Claude de la Colombière was the spiritual director of St. Margaret Mary Alacoque, who received the apparitions of Jesus in which he described his Sacred Heart to her and how to practice that devotion. When St. Margaret Mary asked St. Claude to be her spiritual director, he wanted to test her first. He said to her, "If you are really seeing Jesus, then the next time he appears to you, ask him what my last mortal sin was." The next time they met, he asked her, "Did you see Jesus?"

"Yes," she said.

"Did you ask him what my last mortal sin was?" he asked.

"Yes," she said.

He then pressed further, "Well, what did he say?"

She looked at him and said, "I asked Jesus what your last mortal sin was. He said he forgot."

God's forgiveness of our sins is a letting go of the weight of that burden, but we do not let the burdens go ourselves. We carry the weight of our past with us, letting it pile up over our lifetime. Even if we make acts of forgiveness, or try at times to let go of the mistakes we've made in the past or things we've failed to do, it seems we have a difficult time really letting go of those things permanently. As we journey through life and pick up more responsibilities, love more, give more of ourselves to people and things, we feel even greater weight. Ultimately there is a hint of perfectionism in everyone, and it doesn't let us forget about relationship failures, unresolved arguments, incomplete business, or unrealized dreams. When your thoughts fall into this kind of rut, they don't let go. It almost feels like it would be a sin to let yourself be happy. Many people believe they don't deserve to be happy after what they've done or experienced in life.

It's not just our actual sins that pile up to create this weight. Many of us are taught from the beginning that there is something fundamentally wrong with us. This subtle lesson can be taught through bullying by schoolmates, sibling rivalry, preoccupied or abusive parents, or any number of other distortions in childhood. These thoughts can layer upon each other and create a kind of blanket of shame that covers us. Even when we don't have those specific thoughts racing through our head, we can eventually develop a sense of being wrong or flawed at the deepest level of our being. This is when guilt from doing bad things can turn into a sense of shame in who we are. We feel like a bad person, a bad parent, spouse, child, or friend. We feel like we need to be better at our very core, and we judge ourselves so harshly for having emotions such as anger, bitterness, sadness, or despair. It becomes wrong to enjoy life, and even if we don't consciously think this way, it can become taboo to actually let ourselves off the hook and be happy. Whether you are an introvert or an extrovert, an overachiever or underachiever, there can be an underlying feeling, or a tiny voice whispering to you, "You are not doing enough," "You could do more," "You could be better," and "You don't have the right to be happy."

We can then walk around with an unspoken fear that since we aren't good enough, we are impostors, and that we might be found out. We are afraid of criticism because it means that people know the truth about us. We don't want to let ourselves off the hook because then someone else will put us back on; it's better if we do it to ourselves first. Our belief that we are not good enough causes us to fear rejection and isolation. Because we are born with a deep need to be with other people, we become anxious about ending up alone.

To make matters worse, these thoughts carry with them the added nuance of smelling like permanence. Something about them makes us feel like they will stay forever. When we get trapped into those ruminations, or feel that wet blanket of shame weighing heavy on our shoulders, it feels like it will never change. Sometimes that sense of irreversibility spreads to the ruminations and it makes us feel even worse about ourselves. You can feel hopeless, and each new mistake only cements your despair. This perspective is radically different from the way God sees you.

Generalized Memory

It shouldn't come as a surprise to you at this point that all that thinking, all those feelings, all those patterns are cemented by the doing mode of the autopilot. Research has shown that the autopilot mind has a particular effect on memory and recall. Though more pronounced in some people than in others, it is typically easier to recall specific details of happy memories, while it is more difficult to recall specific details of unhappy ones. If you think about something from your past that makes you happy, what do you think of? Now think of something from your past that makes you unhappy. If you have a particularly frantic mind, are tired, or are prone to depression, research shows that it will be easier for you to paint a vivid, detailed picture of the happy memory but only a generalized sense of the unhappy one. (Trauma itself might be vividly remembered, but that is in a different category.) You might remember a day at the beach from your youth, picturing the waves, the sand, or even the clothes people were wearing. You might still hear the waves and the seagulls, or smell the sunblock. You can feel your toes in the sand. The unhappy memory, how-ever, might be remembered simply as fighting with your brother, or always being in trouble.

The details of a specific unhappy memory or event don't come to mind as easily. It takes much more effort to hold on to those details, and for the most part, it's uncomfortable to do so. Since the mind would rather not sit in that discomfort, it paints the memory with a broad stroke so that you get the gist of what hap-pened, but then it moves on. The mind likes to avoid difficulty.

The problem is, though, the more often people remember in this generalized way, the more difficult it becomes to let go of the past. When you don't remember the details, you can't re-solve them. Often I'll have a patient tell me something like, "I was such a bad kid," or "I never really had friends," or "My sisters never liked me." If I start to probe, it becomes clear that (a) it is difficult to come up with detailed memories to support that narrative, and (b) there is plenty of evidence to disprove it as well. We can live our whole lives with an underlying sense of certain narratives that when examined turn out to be false. Sure, maybe there was conflict with your sisters, and maybe you did get into trouble at times, but those narratives don't include all the good times you actually had, or the accomplishments you were praised for.

These negative generalizations can greatly affect the way we feel about ourselves in the present. Here are some questions to help you discover how you might be carrying a deeper sense of shame and unkindness toward yourself. The way you answer them may indicate that you have generalized a core sense of shame:

- Do you expect more of yourself no matter how much you actually accomplish?
- Do you see yourself as good or bad depending on what thoughts cross your mind?
- Do you tell yourself to stop thinking the thoughts you are thinking?
- Do you consider yourself a perfectionist?
- Do you see yourself as an underachiever, lazy, or a failure?
- Do you tell yourself to stop thinking a certain way, or to stop feeling a certain way?
- Do you feel your thoughts and feelings are inappropriate?

Remember the Thoughts and Sounds exercise. Thoughts, like feelings, come out of nowhere, *without our creating them*, and *outside our control*. You are not responsible for the sounds coming into your ears, and you are not responsible for the initial sparks of thoughts and feelings. You can be responsible for entertaining certain thoughts, which then creates an autopilot association of other thoughts, but the original spark of a thought or feeling you experience is not something to beat yourself up over. If you answered yes to any of the above questions, you are judging yourself for something as unavoidable as your heartbeat. Just as your heart beats, your mind thinks thoughts. Sometimes those thoughts are pretty crazy. When you are carrying the blanket of shame, you look at even those uncontrolled thoughts as somehow your fault.

The good news, as with all effects of the doing mode, is that mindful awareness dissolves the autopilot glue that holds these ruminations and narratives together. As deeply ingrained as they are, these thoughts, feelings, and narratives you carry about yourself are not permanent. It is possible to free yourself from the wet blanket of shame. It is possible to see yourself the way God does. Even when your ruminations try to present all the "evidence" from your past to support the theory that you are unlovable, you can, like God, let go of those things.

Mercy

As you continue to practice mindful awareness, you will develop a new way of relating to yourself. You may have already experienced by this point the ability to sit in a new way with your mind, your thoughts, your memories, your distractions, or whatever else you are experiencing. When you recall difficult and painful experiences, you will still feel the sting, but you can sit with those memories with the full realization that they are *memories*— in other words, something that happened in the past. Instead of feeling as if the object of the painful memories is happening now, being caught in the whirlwind of thoughts and feelings as if you were going through the same situation at this moment, you can have a sort of distance from the mental experience of the memory, realizing you are safe in this present moment.

The autopilot mind sets you up for negativity by generalizing your mistakes or what you've been taught about yourself from your past, locking you into a state of shame and creating a filter that you look through to see the future. Mindfulness dissolves the glue that holds those thoughts together. Each exercise you have practiced thus far has introduced you to a different way of relating to your life—whether it's via a raisin, your body, your breath, a sound, or difficulties you feel or think about. I have been leading you to discover, week by week and moment by moment, that the ways of thinking you assumed were permanently cemented in—just "part of you"—are actually very changeable.

We now progress further, looking at the way you are present to yourself. Of all the things you can be mindful of in your present moment, there is one you will always have: *yourself*. You will be a part of your experience of the present moment forever. Long after your breath has stopped in your current bodily form, long after your ears hear sounds the way they do now or you taste raisins the way you do now, you will still have *you*. Being nonjudgmentally, noncritically, and acceptingly present with yourself can be one of the most difficult exercises to practice, but you have a long time to do so.

Mercy Toward Being vs. Doing

None of this means we can't judge actions. Nonjudgmental awareness does not contradict a need for justice. (Actually, mercy toward ourselves is a form of justice, as we are giving due worship to our Creator—think again about appreciating the artwork of a master painter.) It can sound like we aren't supposed to judge actions, though, and I want to make sure this point is clear: We still judge things that are done. We can judge right and wrong, virtue and vice. Everything we are talking about here is in the realm of being. The goal is to see yourself with the eyes of God, which means to love yourself as God loves you. The disposition of love is the only appropriate response to the *being* of a person. You are lovable, even if you do things at times that are not lovable. You might *do* something bad, but you never *are* bad.

Another manifestation of this question I hear regards the amount of time you are focusing on yourself in this course. Especially when we are thinking about mercy, usually that mercy is something we want to give to others. During the Mercy Exercise introduced in this chapter, you will put that into direct practice. However, you cannot have true mercy toward others if you don't have mercy first toward yourself.

True mercy toward others, as with true forgiveness, requires a Christian disposition. As Christ said, even the sinners love their friends. It is easy to show kindness to people who are kind to us. It is easy to be charitable to those who are agreeable to us. The completely counterintuitive, radical proposal of Christianity, the thing that differs from every other world religion and makes us look like fools according to Scripture, is forgiveness of our enemies.

In order to be able to forgive our enemies, we need to see the way God sees. If we don't see ourselves first the way God sees us, we will not be able to truly see others the way he sees them. We can pretend, or we can muster up some amount of external display of forgiveness, but to truly, deeply, freely find the real flow of charity and mercy that is indicative of real forgiveness, one must see how God sees. This vision is a grace, a freely given gift to God's children who are willing to stop trying to be in control and act as if they don't need a Father. A child who trusts the Father is one who doesn't disregard his disposition. A child who trusts the Father is one who takes his lead, even when it comes to one's own goodness. When you accept yourself with that depth of love, and see yourself with the dignity and honor with which the Father sees you, you are free to receive his grace. When you can first see yourself in this light, you are able to see others in this light. Time spent focusing on yourself, therefore, does not necessitate the elimination of loving others. On the contrary, it will help you love others more.

Some people experience some resistance to the Mercy Exercise and the depth of mercy toward yourself I am proposing here. For instance, part of the Mercy Exercise includes the wish to be free from suffering. This can be extremely triggering for people who don't know how to be kind toward themselves. Many object: "Aren't we supposed to embrace our cross?"

We can find an answer in Scripture:

> Therefore, since we are surrounded by so great a cloud of witnesses, let us also lay aside every weight, and sin which clings so closely, and let us run with perseverance the race that is set before us, looking to Jesus the pioneer and perfecter of our faith, who for the joy that was set before him endured the cross, despising the shame, and is seated at the right hand of the throne of God. (Hebrews 12:1–2)

Let us truly lay aside this weight. Let yourself be at peace knowing that while we do need to accept whatever difficulties and crosses God allows us to suffer, we don't look for them or desire them for their own sake. It is only "for the joy that was set before him" that Jesus endured the cross. The cross is a means to an end, not a good in itself. It is therefore good and holy to pray to not have crosses. It is good and holy to pray to be without suffering. If we are praying for our own conversion, we are praying to someday be without suffering. At the same time, we pray for the grace of acceptance of whatever crosses God does allow in our lives as we trust him to make all things well.

As you begin to practice being with yourself with kindness and mercy, you will discover an even deeper capacity for awareness. You may realize that you are overwhelmed with a sense of busyness. You might discover a feeling that you *should* be busy, or *need* to be busy. You might realize that you feel inadequate if you are not *doing* more. You might then also start to see how this sense is really an act of unkindness toward yourself, a lack of mercy and a deep sense of being unworthy of the gift God has already given. You will realize that these kinds of thoughts, these senses, these narratives are forms of background noise that keep you from hearing the voice of God within you.

Silence

By cultivating mercy toward yourself, you are cultivating a deeper receptivity to silence. It is in silence that you hear the voice of God. It is in silence that you will discover the deepest peace. It is in silence that you will fully find yourself, waking up to the depths of your identity and learning how to live fully alive. It is when you experience this way of living that you realize how unalive you were before.

Silence can also be very uncomfortable for people. In silence you are given the opportunity to encounter yourself, and it is here that whatever issues you might have with yourself come to the surface. The inclination to pull away from this encounter becomes avoidance that we commonly experience as distraction. When we fight through the distraction to be alone in silence, though, the next trick our doing mind employs to make us avoid ourselves is a sense of loneliness. Loneliness is really just an avoidance tactic. It keeps us stuck in an endless cycle of rumination. When we are lonely, there is always a sense that something is wrong, it shouldn't be this way, and it'd be better if something changed. Solitude is the opposite of loneliness. Instead of running from the silent encounter with ourselves, we can turn toward ourselves, confront the loneliness, and let it transform into solitude. Solitude is the place where we meet our true selves with acceptance, which includes the reality that we are made for an infinite Other—we are made to be in relationship with God. The solitude of interior silence then becomes the gateway to meeting God.

Silence, then, is the beginning of a true encounter with God. This is the launching pad that mindfulness can bring you to. Mindfulness is like one of those carts that drive people to their gate at the airport. It is the vehicle we can catch a ride on, instead of struggling to catch our flight. However, it only brings us to the gate. Prayer is sitting on the plane on the runway, and God's grace meets us there, fuels our plane, and takes us into the atmosphere. This book is only meant to be the cart to get you to the gate, but God will meet you in the time you spend in true silence.

First we must realize there is something greater waiting for us on the other side of interior noise. We are barraged by a whirlwind of noise when we take a few minutes to ourselves. Judgments, worries, fears, and a multitude of other distractions prowl in the corners, waiting for us to step into this arena of silence. Cardinal Sarah, in his book *The Power of Silence*,[15] reminds us: "One day, beyond the invasive noise that is perversely interwoven in so many lives, it will be important to listen once again to the 'still small voice,' the voice of God, which will say to us again:

'What are you doing here, Elijah?' (1 Kings 19:12–13)." Let that day be today. He goes on to quote a Carmelite brother who writes:

> Therefore during prayer time it is absolutely necessary to resist the urge to board those trains or boats that go by. In order to do that, it is of capital importance not to identify with these thoughts but, on the contrary, to realize that they come to us, that they are not of us, that they are displayed on the backdrop of our interior silence. That is where we will encounter God. . . . All that he asks of us in his presence is to remain in this silence, which is the most beautiful of all praises that we could offer him.[16]

You can imagine yourself at a transportation terminal while you are exercising mindfulness or even in prayer, in a state of waiting. To begin mindfully, you simply wait at the terminal, letting each train, boat, or plane come and go. Those are your thoughts, beckoning you to board them and let them take you away. Instead, after you acknowledge them, kindly decline the offer and return your focus to the terminal, where you will wait again. If it is God who comes to take you, by all means let him. Cardinal Sarah continues:

> I know it is very difficult to get rid of the manifold problems that can assail us and trouble our silence. How can we ask a mother whose child is seriously ill to hold at bay all the painful thoughts that constantly assail her? How can we ask a man who has just lost his wife, carried off by a long illness, to set aside the veil of sadness that is breaking his heart so as to rediscover a certain quality of silence? Yet even if daily life is as difficult as

it can be, God nevertheless remains present in each one of us. He is a patient, faithful, and merciful God, who waits untiringly. The most difficult thing is probably to come to our senses, to be quiet, to turn towards our Father, to repent and say: "How many of my father's hired servants have bread enough to spare, but I perish here with hunger! I will arise and go to my father, and I will say to him, 'Father, I have sinned against heaven and before you; I am no longer worthy to be called your son; treat me as one of your hired servants.' And he arose and came to his father" (Luke 15:17–20). The journey towards heaven consists of rediscovering our silent interior life in which God dwells and waits for us, watching the horizon.[17]

Cardinal Sarah is comparing the distracting thoughts of a mother with a sick child or a husband who lost his wife to the Prodigal Son! Yet at the heart of all worry, all anxiety, is a distrust in God's loving care for us. Like the Prodigal Son, we will run to our Father when we trust that living under his care is better than living outside that reality, which is where we go when we worry and forget that he will make all things well. When we turn our hearts and mind back to God with a disposition of peaceful trust, we find him waiting for us.

EXERCISES

Mercy Exercise

You may feel at times that you are not doing a good enough job with the mindfulness practices. You may grow angry or frustrated with yourself as you realize you aren't living up to a preconceived notion of what mindfulness "success" looks like. You may think you should be reaching a state of thoughtless awareness, or otherwise sit without distraction during the exercises. These notions about mindfulness are not accurate. Even if you find yourself getting upset with yourself for "not being mindful enough," realize that this is not the disposition of mercy that God wants you to cultivate toward yourself—it is not his disposition toward you. The judgments that arise in the mind while practicing, however, can serve to illuminate more about the way your mind works. As you think these thoughts, you may also feel tension in your shoulders, frustration in your head or face, or an anxious heartbeat. Instead of seeing these physical signs as symptoms of failure, realize that you are *aware* of them now, in a new way. This awareness itself is a significant discovery and a mark of progress. The simple act of being aware derails the autopilot and the consequent physical manifestations of its power.

Pick a consistent time twice a day that generally works for you. It is especially helpful to practice before times of prayer. You can also pray the novena found at the end of the book after one of your practices each day.

- Call to mind the presence of God: "Ever-present God, here with me now, help me to be here with you."

- Settle in, relaxed and alert. Find a position that is most comfortable, where you can sit with yourself in the presence of God. Be aware of your dignity. You are the son or daughter of the great high King, of the Father who is the Creator of all that is. He loves you. He created you. You are precious to him. Embody this dignity.
- Focus on your breath. While breathing in and out, expand your attention to your whole body, until you feel truly present to this moment. Take a moment to do this now.
o When your mind wanders, acknowledge where it's going, remembering that you have a choice now: either to escort it back to whatever you had intended to focus on or to allow your attention to drop into your body to explore where you are experiencing the trouble or concern.
- When you are ready, allow the following phrases to come to your mind (these thoughts are the gateway to a compassion and mercy toward yourself; they are a way to befriend yourself):
  - May I be free from suffering.
  - May I be as healthy and happy as it is possible for me to be.
  - May I be at peace.
- Taking your time, imagine that each phrase is a pebble being dropped into a deep well. You are dropping each one in turn, listening to any reaction of thoughts, feelings, bodily sensations, or an impulse to act. There is no need to judge what arises. Simply be aware of it.
- Bring a sense of friendship, compassion, and mercy toward yourself. Should this be difficult, call to mind a friendship with a person who, either in the past or present, has loved

you unconditionally. Think of this person; think of his or her love for you. See if you can return to offering this same love to yourself.

- May I be free from suffering.
- May I be as happy and healthy as possible.
- May I be at peace.

- Next bring to mind a loved one and wish well to that person in the same way.

  - May he or she be free from suffering.
  - May he or she be as happy and healthy as possible.
  - May he or she be at peace.

- Once again see what arises in your body as you hold this person in your mind and heart. Allow these responses to come. Take your time and pause between saying these phrases to yourself, listening attentively to what is happening inside you.

- Next choose a stranger whom you may have crossed paths with. Just like you, she has hopes and dreams, wounds and fears. She too wishes to be happy, just like you. Keeping this person in your heart and mind, repeat the phrases of well-wishing. Allow yourself to cultivate a deep sense of mercy, charity, and love for this person. As you repeat these words, see if you can feel warmth toward this person.

- Now bring to mind someone you find difficult, from your past or present. Allow him to be in your heart and mind, acknowledging that he too wishes to be happy, and to be free from suffering. Again repeat the phrases:

  - May he be free from suffering.
  - May he be happy and healthy.
  - May he be at peace.

- Gently listen to your body, your thoughts, your sensations. Explore these feelings with curiosity, awareness, and openness, without censoring or judging yourself.
- If at any time you feel overwhelmed, you can always come back to your breath to anchor yourself in the present moment. Then when you're ready, move back toward a position of kindness and mercy.
- Finally, think of all the people who have been on your mind and in your heart. Extend this loving-kindness and compassionate mercy to all of them, including the loved ones, the stranger, the one you find most difficult to love, and yourself. Extend this mercy, kindness, and love to all people.
  - May all be free from suffering.
  - May all be happy and healthy.
  - May all of us be at peace.
- At the end of this practice, take time to sit with your breath and body, resting in clear awareness of the present moment. As you continue to practice this exercise, you may experience different levels of difficulty or ease, distraction or resistance. But sit in gratitude, thanking God for this time. Cultivate gratitude for the chance to experience a sense of curiosity, openness, and awareness that is part of being a child of God, of having a Father who loves you.

Sacramental Pause

Continue to practice this exercise twice per day. Additionally, you can use it anytime you feel you are starting to ruminate or some worry is sweeping your focus away.

Advanced version: This week, spend some time with your thoughts and feelings after the last part of the exercise. Try to have a different relationship to any negative thoughts or feelings you might have. Distance yourself from them by labeling them or becoming aware of the filters or narratives you have that lead to those negative thoughts.

Habit Disrupter: Mercy Toward Self and Others

This week the habit disrupter consists of two different activities:

1. Mercy Toward Self: Let your mind go to a time in your life that has a particularly happy feeling around it, and think about something specific you used to do during that time. This might be something you did in college when you had more free time, or something you did when you first met your spouse. Find a way this week to reengage with that activity. Plan a specific time when you will do so.

2. Mercy Toward Others: Perform a random act of kindness for someone else this week. It doesn't matter if it is someone you know or a stranger. Mindfully pick some recipient for this gift of kindness, and perform the act in secret.

CHAPTER SEVEN

Restoring Balance

*Let nothing disturb you. Let nothing make you afraid. All things
are passing. God alone never changes. Patience gains all things.
If you have God, you will want for nothing. God alone suffices.*
—St. Teresa of Ávila

It doesn't happen overnight. You don't realize the extent to which
it is happening, even though there are times when you might
catch a glimpse. When you do see it, you figure it will get better
on its own, that this is just temporary and there's nothing to seriously work on changing. I'm referring to *imbalance*.

Children's lives are mostly carefree. They worry about what
games they will play, but most of life for them is a game. We all
start off with that playfulness, and with curiosity and excitement
about the world. We began with dreams about what life would
be like when we grew up, and never imagined what paying bills,
taxes, and insurance premiums felt like. We didn't know there
were so many responsibilities, and we didn't realize just how easy
it would be to lose that playful curiosity. Little by little, over the
span of a lifetime, the seriousness of life's responsibilities takes
over and we end up running the rat race instead of really living
life.

Whatever your vocation or role in life, you carry the weight of responsibility on your shoulders. In every stage of life as you emerge from childhood, you bear that weight. It makes sense that there are things to take seriously, other people who count on you, and a future that depends on choices you make now.

It is precisely because your future depends on choices you make now that you need to look more clearly at the amount of balance in your life. Most people are going through life blindly: "They don't make an instruction manual for this." That's actually a more recent (and unfortunate) saying. There used to be communities of families with elderly members living in close proximity to younger members. The path to manhood or womanhood was well paved, the milestones and expectations were clear, and there was a whole community of people cheering you on, picking you up when you fell, teaching you along the way, and admonishing you when you went off the path. Now the twenties are the worst decade of life development in terms of symptoms of anxiety and depression. "Midlife crisis" is statistically no longer the most difficult life stage; it is now "emerging adulthood." A person's life in his or her twenties can be the most tumultuous time of the entire life span.

Whether you passed through that period long ago or have yet to do so, you can open your eyes to a new way of seeing. God does not want us to lose our playfulness. Even though there are responsibilities that he expects us to carry out, he even went so far as to say, "Truly I say to you, unless you turn and become like children, you will never enter the kingdom of God" (Matthew 18:3). In that verse, Jesus was referring to the humility of a child, but humility requires the sense that there is someone else in charge. It requires trust, which can be seen in the playfulness of a child. A child is carefree because someone else is taking care of the responsibilities. This is even more clear if you've ever seen children who've been traumatized, abused, or living in deep poverty. When the basic needs of life are not provided, childhood is much less playful. In our adulthood, we tend to act more like those deprived children, even though we have the intellect and faith to believe that God provides what is necessary at all times and in all places.

Spiraling Toward Despair

Losing trust, carefree playfulness, and curiosity is a slow process. We can see periods of our life when this might have happened, and some people are stuck in a narrative in which this can describe their whole life. It is helpful to use the image of a spiraling funnel. We can be like marbles that are spinning around inside the funnel, slowly making our way down to the spout. At the top, we slowly circle around, feeling tired and experiencing sleeplessness (or sometimes pervasive drowsiness). We feel the discomfort of things not going right, but we think we just need to work a little harder at solving our problems, try a little harder to think things through, or keep persisting a little more with the same old coping skills we've used our whole life ("Just let it go; things will get better."). That fatigue, though, can turn to irritability as we spin farther down the spiral, and we may feel physical symptoms of discomfort as our body warns us that something is wrong. People can live a long time in this kind of state, trying to make little changes here and there, eating differently, exercising, trying to change superficial things in their life. Other people are assumed to be the problem, or we might maintain the same old inner narratives that tell us that we are the problem. As the marble keeps rolling, eventually we can drop down into a feeling of hopelessness, joylessness, and despair.

We maintain the normal life at the top of the spiral by keeping a healthy balance between activities that nurture us and those that deplete us. When we get busy, we tend to enter more quickly into the doing mode, problem solving and trying to make ourselves less busy. This typically means doing more of the work that actually depletes us, and less of the kinds of activities that nurture us. We sacrifice doing things we like for things we assume (usually blindly, in autopilot mode) we need to do to "solve the problem." As we spiral down and find that our mood hasn't changed, we feel even more frantic, and we have more problems to solve, so we double down on how we handle our stress and work harder to solve the problems. We speed down the spiral as we narrow our experience of life to focus on solving immediate problems in our mind instead of seeing the big picture. A lot of people are walking around in a fog of low-grade depression because of this behavior. The following list of symptoms can point out if you or someone you know is in this category:

- Increasing irritability or bad moods
- Diminishing social life, loss of a desire to see people
- Diminishing motivation to deal with life's responsibilities such as paying bills, grocery shopping, cleaning, laundry, or routine work requirements
- Feeling fatigued or exhausted easily
- Letting go of healthy exercise
- Missing deadlines or canceling appointments
- Sleeplessness or extreme drowsiness
- Unintentional changes in eating habits

If this list hits close to home, you are headed down the spiral. If you were to keep going in the same direction without making the correct changes, it would be only a matter of time before you ended up in despair.

Nourishing and Depleting Activities

Our life is made up of daily routines and happenings. When we brush our teeth, make breakfast, or drive to work, we don't typically think about that as our life, but it is. Every interaction with another person is part of what makes up our life. Is life good? Is life difficult? These are big questions that we can push off because we might not think we have time for that kind of reflection. The reality is, though, that the conversations we have with the cashier at the grocery store, the doorman, or our neighbors' kids as they leave for school in the morning make up life. It's how we walk, how we drive, how we eat, and how we relate to others. Life is good when our moments are good. At least, life is good when there is a balance to our moments.

It turns out that we can look at those daily moments and figure out if they are nourishing or depleting us of energy and peace. There are many kinds of moments and ways of experiencing them that build us up, increase our peace, and strengthen our resilience against losing it. Other moments tend to rob our peace, stripping us of our energy, attention, curiosity, or joy. These moments weaken our resilience and make us vulnerable to the ruminations that come from autopilot problem solving.

I want to introduce you to a practical way to evaluate the moments of your typical day. I refer to this as the Balance Sheet. Run through the activities that are a part of a normal day for you. Really take a few moments to do this, thinking through a typical day and breaking it down into moments. Be as specific as you can. "Getting the kids ready" might include waking them up, getting them dressed, preparing breakfast, brushing teeth, and so on. "Work" might include the different aspects of the commute, whom you greet or speak with when you arrive, getting coffee, setting yourself up, and so on.

After spending five or ten minutes thinking through a typical day, write the activities down on the Life Activities Balance Sheet in the left column. Then think about which activities nourish you. These are the moments that lift your mood, make you feel calm and peaceful, and can give you energy and motivation. They are the moments when you are your best. Look down your list and put an "N" in the right column next to each activity or moment that is nourishing.

Next think about which moments deplete you. These are the ones that can rob you of peace, zap your energy, or drain your motivation. They can be moments of possible tension, or moments that you simply coast through, existing in but not really being alive or awake to. Mark a "D" next to those activities. If you can't decide whether to mark an activity as depleting or nourishing, or if it can be either depending on the day, mark them both, with the predominant letter first ("D/N" or "N/D").

Life Activities Balance Sheet

Activity	Nourishing (N) or Depleting (D)

Activity	Nourishing (N) or Depleting (D)
1.	
2.	
3.	
4.	
5.	

After you have evaluated each activity, tally up the N's and D's at the bottom of the page. If you marked both, only count the first letter (we are looking for trends here, not precision). This will give you an idea of what a typical day's balance is for you, and you can use it to understand why you feel the way you feel at this point in your life. If you feel frantic, stressed, behind, or deep down not good enough, inadequate, or even unloved, you can find a corollary here. How you spend your day affects how you feel.

This chart can be a tremendously powerful tool to uncover patterns of the doing mode in your life. It will help you discover the keys that will unlock the full potential to be mindful and move toward deeper peace. You can now take action with these points and the map in general. You may decide that you need to add things to your day that bring more moments of nourishing awareness to your life. You might also realize that you can change how you are disposed to the very things on that list. Almost every D can be turned into an N. It's not the activity that dictates how you respond to it; it's your interpretation of the activity. You can practice being fully present to those activities that you find depleting, even if they are uncomfortable, boring, or otherwise distasteful. Often, simply leaving more time to accomplish the depleting activity is enough to turn it into an N. Finding those depleting spots ahead of time will show you where to manage your time better. It also would be good to go through this exercise with someone you know and trust.

Elizabeth, who runs a company, used this approach to evaluate her daily activities. With the help of a mentor, she discovered she was spending too much time looking at numbers. She was anxious about the bottom line and the pressure she felt from the company's board, and so she revisited sales and expenses many times throughout the day. She realized she only really needed to look at those numbers once a week, and if there were other issues that required attention, she had a team to point them out. Most people do the same thing with email. How many times do you think you truly need to check your phone during the day? How many times do you actually check your phone during the day? I bet those two numbers are very different.

How much time is wasted on Facebook or other social media? Most people call those things a "guilty pleasure." Depleting yourself of positivity certainly isn't pleasurable. If you didn't include Internet usage on your list of activities, it will be helpful to go back and add it. How much time do you spend a day on the Internet? If you need help figuring this out, there is a great little program called RescueTime that you can run for free on your computer or phone (www.rescuetime.com). It will track all the time you spend on different websites or email. If you don't have time for nourishing activities (such as mindfulness exercises, for example) but you do have time for Facebook, you may want to reconsider how you are choosing to spend your time and to what end each of those activities leads.

As you begin to add N's to your day, or convert D's to N's, you will find your day changing. Not only that, but you will find there is more time throughout the day that you previously considered nonexistent. Part of being mired in the doing mode is the tendency to broadly sweep a judgment over the whole day. "This day is just too hectic." "I'm really in a rut." "Next week will be better." Instead, moments of being mode can squeeze open more moments in those very days that were previously considered hectic. The whole day is never actually hectic. Even if you just count times going to the bathroom, you can find a few minutes here and there. The kids don't let you go to the bathroom, you say? There are moments. Everyone has moments.

At the end of the Balance Sheet there are a few open lines. Write down five concrete actions you are going to take to shift the balance of N's and D's. They can include adding specific nourishing activities, or ways to change your relationship with specific depleting activities. Either way, write them down. If you are serious about changing the way you feel and putting the trust you have in God into real action in your life, writing this list is essential. You can come back to it later, and revisit it every week or so to see how the map has changed. Over time you can rebalance your life, feeling more nourished and less depleted.

The Autopilot Aversion

Of course, your autopilot mind is not going to like this kind of exercise. If you thought it took too much time out of your very important and hectic day before to simply sit and listen to a recorded mindfulness exercise or to practice it on your own, there's almost certainly not enough time to sit and write lists and think about your day in a broad sense. Remember, the autopilot is operating as if your life is in danger. When you are running from danger, you don't need the best escape route, just the quickest. If the building you are in is on fire, you might jump from a high window or off the roof—not the best exit, but certainly the quickest. The autopilot brain doesn't work with what's best; it works with what's most immediate. Taking time away from doing the dishes, laundry, or payroll in order to just think about those activities does not seem like an immediate solution. Your autopilot, doing mind will try to keep you away from this exercise.

Your mind might tell you, "I have so many things on my plate, there just isn't enough time to do this now." "Is this really worth my time?" or "If I don't keep up with all my obligations, I'll fall behind. I'll get to this later." You might also think, "I can do something that's good for me once I've finished everything else on the list; it will be my reward." Realistically, though, that point will never come. You might tell yourself, "This is just the way it is; there are certain things in life you just have to accept." Ironically, this is the opposite of acceptance, as it is the doing mind actually avoiding making a change. Another example I hear all the time, especially in a religious context: "I think this is making me focus too much on myself—aren't we supposed to be thinking about others and less of ourselves?"

When these thoughts arise, they provide yet another opportunity to turn mindfully toward them. You can recognize them as mental objects, creations of the doing mind that invite you to turn on the being mind. If you blindly follow them, you only continue to engage the autopilot, but if you turn toward them, hear and study them, notice their character (especially how black-and-white they are, without seeming to leave any room for gray), you can turn the moment into a mindful one. God is calling to you. He wants you to know how precious you are, and he wants your sense of self to be transformed by that knowledge. He will help you use whatever material possible at whatever point you decide to turn things around. If you find yourself lost in ruminations for twenty minutes but then have a moment of coming to your senses, you can use that one moment to totally free yourself from the previous twenty.

Almost every sense of stress, fatigue, or unhappiness comes with the notion that it will never go away. There is a tone of permanence to the voice of unhappiness. When we don't look directly at those thoughts as thoughts, we let them convince us of their permanence. When we turn toward them, we can see that they can quickly disappear or their chains can be dissolved. Adding in nourishing moments also helps you to discover the trend of your mood on a given day. You can more easily discover when you are headed down the spiral, and you'll know which activities to turn to or make time for that will nourish you.

Adding Action to the Sacramental Pause: PERMA

I've been introducing the Sacramental Pause to you in stages so that you can get the hang of what it is supposed to be at its core. Once you become skilled at this exercise and can step into being mode, you can get more out of it. The next stage is to implement an action item after the pause. Even though *doing* was a bad word in the beginning of the book, it is necessary that we do things in our life, and it is helpful to know exactly what to do to increase your peace in any given moment.

Martin Seligman is a psychologist and a past president of the American Psychological Association. After researching the behavioral mode he labeled "learned helplessness," which is basically a description of the way we build negative narratives into our autopilot and operate based on them without reevaluating them in the present moment, he decided he needed to do something a little more positive. In fact, Seligman ended up pioneering a whole new branch of psychology called *positive psychology*. Instead of studying people with disorders and figuring out their common denominators, he chose to study people who are *happy* and study *their* common denominators. His book *Flourish* describes this work.[18] He discovered there are five main areas of growth in a person's life that contribute to a sense of flourishing. When an individual has developed these five areas, he or she is also resilient to suffering the long-standing effects of trauma when bad things happen in life. Seligman coined the acronym PERMA to describe the five categories:

- Positive Emotion
- Engagement
- Relationships
- Meaning
- Accomplishment

These also represent five ways you can take action at the end of a Sacramental Pause. Once you have gone through the three steps, decide which one of the following five actions you will take:

Positive emotion describes the ability of a person to take care of the body. This kind of positive treatment of the self through the body is properly ordered in a Christian worldview. God made our bodies good, and it is good to experience pleasure through them. This would include things like taking a hot bath, having a nice glass of wine, and going for a pleasant walk. *Anhedonia* literally means "without pleasure," and it is one of the symptoms of depression. As you spiral down toward despair, you lose the ability to experience pleasure. Taking time out to create pleasurable moments is healthy and good for you. This might be what you choose to do after your Sacramental Pause.

Engagement refers to the type of activity that you fully enjoy. This is when you do something, often a hobby, for its own enjoyment. It is something you feel you are made for; there is a resonance in your spirit when you engage in it, and you could do it for hours without keeping track of the time. After a Sacramental Pause, you might decide to set up a time when you can reconnect with a hobby or activity that replenishes you in this way.

Positive relationships is exactly what it sounds like. We are made for relationships, so engaging in healthy ones is an important factor in flourishing. This means there are appropriate understandings of boundaries in different kinds of relationships, and we have friendships that are mutually beneficial. Your mindful action might be a decision about how to move a relationship in a positive direction. If you did the Sacramental Pause because of an interpersonal conflict, this can be a particularly helpful path to decide to take.

Meaning describes having a worldview in which there is a greater significance to life. This necessarily includes a sense of someone or something in the universe that is bigger than we are. It is very consistent with the whole premise of Catholic mindfulness as I've presented it here. We need to know that the weight of the universe doesn't rest on our shoulders, and once we do, we can walk a little lighter. Your mindful action might be to reconnect with God, taking the prayer of his presence a step further. You might pray the Divine Mercy chaplet if you have time, or simply end with, "Jesus, I trust in you."

Accomplishment means you have goals you set for yourself that require discipline and sacrifice, which you can work toward and reach. When you arrive at those goals, you feel a sense of accomplishment that contributes to an overall sense of flourishing. Often we feel overwhelmed because the goals we set for ourselves are too lofty. Instead, it is very helpful to break larger goals down into smaller ones. Instead of cleaning the whole house, you can just clean the kitchen. Instead of cleaning the whole kitchen, you might just empty out the sink. Your mindful action might be to accomplish a reachable goal.

The Sacramental Pause opens up the possibility of making a tiny change in your day that will have significant effects. Very often, when we need motivation the most, we have it the least. This is because, as mentioned earlier, the doing mode tries to get things done in the easiest way possible. It tries to find the path of least resistance, the one that doesn't require motivation. Many times this path is also producing unhappiness, stress, fatigue, and anxiety. Those are the times you need to make a change. Instead of waiting to "feel" motivated, you often have to force yourself to get the ball rolling without feeling it. It turns out that if you can at least have enough awareness to hit the reset button, motivation will slowly emerge to keep it going. This is what the Sacramental Pause offers you. If you set an alarm or have a regular time to practice it, you will find the space, even if just for a moment, to make a tiny change. It might be taking a short walk, sipping a cup of tea, or listening to a song you enjoy. These activities will be unique to you, and it doesn't matter what they are as long as they help you reconnect with the present.

Mindfulness Triggers

Now that you have a better sense of what mindfulness is, you can look more and more for ways to integrate it into your daily life. While the formal exercises will always be beneficial, it is also helpful to have ways to practice mindfulness "on the fly." One way to remember to practice is to set reminders or alarms for yourself on your phone. You can create a custom ringtone or vibration that specifically tells you it's time to be mindful. Even if you just keep your phone in your pocket, let the alarm bring you back to your senses, and continue doing whatever you are doing in a mindful way, you will have reconnected to your being mind. One priest I worked with used a church bell ringtone to remind him periodically to practice a Sacramental Pause. In times past, the church bells were meant to give people periodic reminders to turn their attention to the presence of God, so this was certainly an appropriate way to use the phone!

You can also develop associations with normal parts of your day that are already there. Go back to your Balance Sheet and look at the activities that are currently depleting for you. You can pick something about each one that will help remind you to be mindful. For me, driving is always a source of tension and anxiety. I'm easily swept away by traffic down some thought stream. I wrote an extra D next to that item when it first showed up on my own Balance Sheet. I've set the feeling of the steering wheel in my mind as a mindfulness trigger. Now when I get in the car and feel the steering wheel, it reminds me to pay attention to my senses. I notice its texture, its softness or hardness, and am simply aware of the sensations created in the sensory neurons of my fingers and hands as I hold it. I let that awareness expand to the rest of my body as I sit in the seat, feel the pedals, and then listen to the sounds around me. Instead of experiencing a depleting commute, I can often turn my drive into a mindfulness exercise and start off every day from a mindful place. Imagine what possibilities lie ahead when you begin your day with an open mind that is primed to operate at its most creative and efficient. You will quickly learn that many moments every day invite you to focus on the present moment and to reconnect with what is real, here and now, so that you can fully wake up and stop half-living in autopilot mode. You will find you reverse out of the spiral of despair and discover within yourself a deep sense of abiding peace, the peace God desires for you.

EXERCISES

Revisiting
Practice two exercises from the previous chapters. They can be practiced back-to-back or separately throughout the day, but practice them each once per day.

- Choose one exercise that was particularly nourishing for you, that you enjoyed, or that you felt you were able to stay present with most fully.
- Choose one exercise you had a particularly difficult time with, that you did not enjoy, or that you felt you were not able to stay present with.

Sacramental Pause + PERMA Action
Continue to practice the Sacramental Pause twice per day. Additionally, you can use it anytime you feel you are starting to ruminate or some worry is sweeping your focus away.

Choose one of the PERMA categories (Positive Emotion, Engagement, Relationships, Meaning, Achievement) that you are able to act on in the moment following your Sacramental Pause, even if only to make a decision about something you will do later.

Habit Disrupter: Change "D" to "N"

Pick one of the activities you listed on your Balance Sheet as a depleting activity (D) and plan to spend a few extra minutes with that activity so that you can turn it into a nourishing activity. Taking a few deep, mindful breaths, doing a Sacramental Pause, or saying a quick prayer before doing something depleting is a good way to help your mind stay focused on the present moment and turn it into a nourishing act for you.

CHAPTER EIGHT

Waking Up

Rejoice in the Lord always; again I will say, Rejoice. . . . Have no anxiety about anything, but in everything by prayer and supplication with thanksgiving let your requests be made known to God. And the peace of God, which passes all understanding, will keep your hearts and your minds in Christ Jesus.
—Philippians 4:4, 6–7

Your life is precious. You are precious. You are more valuable than diamonds and gold, more valuable than all the riches in the world. You are made in the image of God and destined for eternity. Your deepest being, as you are, as you sit now in the present moment and encounter yourself, will never cease to exist. Your life will only continue to move forward, and eventually you will pass from this existence to the next. Nothing in your wildest dreams can prepare you for what lies ahead. It is like we are returned to a state within our mother's womb, totally unable to comprehend what life looks like after birth. Our world now is another kind of womb, and our death will be a passing through to life in a totally new world. That is the kind of being you are—one destined for happiness and joy beyond your wildest imagination.

Every breath you take is a holy one, sanctified by the Word made flesh that breathed with the same kind of lungs through the same kind of nose. Focus for a moment on that breath, reconnect with yourself, and reconnect with what is holy.

It is far too easy in our state to lose this sense of the sacred. Do you ever just sit and enjoy the accomplishments you have achieved in your life? Or do you have a perpetual sense of not-yet, the feeling that real achievement is waiting for you just around the corner? If so, you will never round that corner, because you are really going in circles.

It is time for you to awaken. Open your eyes, breathe, and feel your whole self. Here you are, complete right now. This is not new age fluff; this is the reality of the Incarnation. Jesus Christ is God in the flesh, and you have the same flesh. Your humanity is sanctified, and you will find peace when you wake up to that reality.

There is actually a lot to do here in this world, but it is not the kind of achievement that we often think. Our one task, our one goal, the whole purpose, meaning, and secret of our lives, is to learn how to fully trust God. Trusting God is everything. Abandoning ourselves to him as a child to a father is the only goal that matters. We should have a healthy kind of anxiety that drives us on toward deeper and deeper abandonment. This is the kind of anxiety that immediately resolves itself as soon as we are aware of it, because when we are aware of the solution to our anxiety, we can immediately embrace it. Total surrender is the solution. It is the secret to happiness and holiness. It is the only thing that matters when it comes to living for sainthood, and it is a solution that is actually possible to obtain.

I think it makes sense that God allows bad things to happen so that we can learn to trust him more. Bad things are always going to happen. Every one of us is going to die, and some of us in terribly tragic ways at tragic times. The point is, though, that staying alive is not the goal. While we do have a duty to protect the life God gave us in every way possible, ultimately we all pass through death to whatever is waiting for us on the other side. Staying alive is not the goal of life, even though our bodies operate as if it were. We find within ourselves this "survival instinct" native to our bodies, but we can learn how to use it appropriately instead of overusing it when our lives aren't even in danger. Ultimately we can even learn to transform the survival instinct to move us toward the highest goal—not of staying alive but of trusting God. That is when we can become anxious about surrender. Do we trust God enough? Can we give him more? What are you holding on to? Let it go right now. Don't hold on to anything. There is nothing that you are holding on to that is safer in your hands than in God's. Even if you don't understand what he is doing with the things you give him, they will be better off in his hands. Even if it looks like death is winning, it never does. He has already conquered even death. Take heart.

Freedom is the heart of dignity. It is not always fully available to us, however, and it can be restricted by bad choices, disease, or ignorance. Bad choices need to be corrected through confession and spiritual direction. Diseases are treated by appropriate doctors. The lack of knowledge is "healed" by education. Throughout this book you have learned new ways to engage more of your freedom. You have learned that your thoughts are not you, and you can develop an entirely different kind of relationship to them.

Embracing Freedom

The irony of the doing mind is that it gives us a sense of control over our life, when in reality, it is keeping our control asleep. There are times in life when it seems that things are slowly unraveling. This is when stress and anxiety can be overwhelming. Fatigue, irritability, and sadness may permeate much of your day. You might feel that it's only a matter of a few steps before you lose it or slip into depression or self-destructive behavior. The truth is, though, that unhappiness is not a cloud that surrounds us; it is not a free-floating affliction. Stress doesn't just come out of nowhere, and the world is not against us. Stress and anxiety are caused not by life, but by the way we relate to our thoughts and feelings, to each other, and to the world around us. Those feelings are the signals that God gave us to let us know that something is wrong *within* us that can be changed.

This is your choice. When you accept the reality that you can make a change in how you feel by changing the way you relate to yourself, other people, and the world around you, totally new possibilities open up for you. You realize that your mind is capable of so much more, but it is extremely limited when it is in the doing mode. Your freedom to focus on the present moment melts those limitations away, and you experience peace. It then becomes so clear that you were made to have this peace. Your heart resonates in these moments, and deeper than your thoughts and feelings, you experience the presence of God. He is the source of that peace, and he is here, waiting for us, in each moment.

Here is a list of ten methods you can use to implement mindfulness in your daily life.

1. **Heroic minute:** St. Josemaría Escrivá inspired a practice to help start the day off right:

Conquer yourself each day from the very first moment, getting up on the dot, at a fixed time, without yielding a single minute to laziness. If, with God's help, you conquer yourself, you will be well ahead for the rest of the day.... The heroic minute. It is the time fixed for getting up. Without hesitation: a supernatural reflection and ... up! The heroic minute: here you have a mortification that strengthens your will and does no harm to your body.[19]

This is a great practice and one that can start your day off with a bit of mindfulness. Staying in bed awake first thing in the morning can be a significant source of rumination for a lot of people. Instead, try setting an alarm and jumping up as soon as you are awake. A lot of times what makes this more difficult are the thoughts about getting your day started. You might not be ready to begin your morning routine just yet. The heroic minute doesn't require that; in fact, you wouldn't be starting mindfully if you just launched into your morning autopilot routine. Try getting out of bed and sitting on the floor. Give yourself permission to take a few minutes just for yourself. Ruminating in bed is unhealthy, because even though you feel like you are resting a bit just for yourself, you are actually setting yourself up with an anxious start to your day. When you get out of bed, sit on the floor and take a few moments to breathe and be fully alive to the present moment—you are waking up the best way possible.

2. **Regular sacramental pauses:** Punctuate your day with regular breaks. This is a simplified and layperson-appropriate

version of what religious and priests do by praying the Liturgy of the Hours (Morning Prayer, Evening Prayer, etc.). While praying the Liturgy of the Hours might be nice at times when you can fit it in, one of the benefits of regular prayer is that it creates a kind of cadence or rhythm to your daily life. This is not achieved by doing something only occasionally. A sacramental pause can be done every day, no matter what state of life you are in. It takes discipline to make it a habit, but it is not impossible. Use your phone to set notifications, reminders, or alarms to go off a couple of times a day to remind you to take a break from the busyness and reconnect with yourself and the presence of God.

3. **Emergency sacramental pauses:** Use the sacramental pause as needed. This is not meant to be a fix to your anxiety, stress, irritability, or any other emotion. It is simply a way to give yourself the freedom to choose how you are going to move forward in your day when it is being overcome by the doing mind. Turn off your autopilot by stepping out for a minute when it is really hurting you.

4. **Catholic mindfulness exercises:** The exercises you've learned in this book will be available to you at www.catholicmindfulness.com/audio, and you should use them regularly. If there's an exercise that you found particularly beneficial, go back to it. Use it every day. They are all a little different because they are meant to teach you different aspects of mindful awareness, but each one is mindfulness itself. More courses and exercises will be added over time, so be sure to stay in touch.

5. **Maintain mercy toward yourself:** Take some time each day for yourself. Find five or ten minutes daily to spend with yourself as if you were visiting a masterpiece in a museum. You are infinitely more valuable than the most expensive painting. Remember that your thoughts and feelings are not you. You don't have to judge yourself for the mental and emotional events that occur within you. You have learned to accept yourself as you are, sensing the deep goodness and beauty of your own being. Let your overall disposition toward yourself continue to be formed by this deepest sense of self. Grow in your appreciation of yourself as one who honors a work of art created by a masterful artist. Only when you come to see yourself as a masterpiece do you truly appreciate the Creator.

6. **Mindful living:** As you learned through exercises such as the Mindful Walk, you can bring mindfulness to normal daily events. You can change the way you walk, ride a train, wait in line, shop for groceries, or play with your kids. You can eat differently, work differently, and have conversations differently. Pick a couple of things you do every day and make a commitment to yourself to turn them into your daily mindfulness exercises. The beauty of mindfulness is that it is not just another task to accomplish in your day. It may feel that way at times as you are working through this book because you are still learning what mindfulness is, but it doesn't mean that it is something you separate from the rest of your life. Imagine if you could go to a class at the local gym to learn how to change walking into the best physical exercise you would ever need. You could get in the

best shape of your life just by changing the way you walk. That is essentially what you are learning how to do here for mental health. You could have the most peace in your life simply by learning how to change the way you do all the things you already do.

7. **Increase exercise:** Many people think they don't have time to live their life, figure out how to eat well, go to the gym, and then add mindfulness exercises on top of everything else. Physical activity such as going to the gym or an exercise class, walking outside, or even something as simple as working around the house or gardening can be done mindfully. We are required to be physically active less and less, and in this process of technological advancement, we are losing touch with everything around us. Every once in a while, make things a little more physically challenging for yourself instead of easier.

8. **Reduce technology use:** Most people use technology more than they need to. Convenience is addicting, and our brains are no match for the way gadgets have permeated our lives. Try to take an ounce of control back in your life by removing one or two ways that you overuse technology. You can limit the time the TV is on, limit how often you check your smartphone, restrict emailing to a certain time of the day, delete apps from your phone that you don't really need, or even trade your smartphone in for a "dumb" one. While these things might sound radical and totally countercultural, I promise that you will never meet a person who has done these things and found them to be not worth it.

9. **Breathe:** The breath of God created the world. Breath is a symbol of life. For our purposes here, it is a continuous reminder that you are alive. Your breath is one of the most practical mindfulness exercises, because it is constantly shifting and always with you. It is simply easier to pay attention to things that are shifting instead of things that are still. By focusing your attention on the gentle fluctuations of your breath, you open the space in your mind to rest in the quiet stillness of the present moment. Some days a mindful breath is the best you can do, and that is enough.

10. **Balance map:** Return often to the Life Activities Balance Sheet. Every week, or at least once a month, rewrite your list and see how your balance is moving in the direction of nourishment. You can use this sheet as a map that will plot the course of your life in the direction of greater peace.

These are simple things to try to keep in mind as you move forward. You might even make a note card to carry with you. Choose three of the ten ways to implement mindfulness that are most effective for you, write them on the back of a business card, and keep it in your wallet. Whatever you do, keep practicing.

It is also helpful to decide what motivating reason is worth your time and energy. While you have been progressing through this book, is there any one particular part of your life that has really improved? Have there been moments when you felt like a better spouse, a better parent, or a better neighbor? How have you become a better version of yourself while working through this book? Spend a few moments considering that question. Ask yourself if it is worth it to maintain your practice and keep moving forward for that reason. Ultimately your own relationship with God is affected by your trustful abandonment, so that can be the deepest motivating factor. Depending on where you are in life, though, it might be very reasonable (and perfectly acceptable) that keeping your kids in mind, for example, will be a stronger practical motivation. Whatever the reasons, find them and keep going.

Your peace will continue to increase as you see yourself and the world more in the way God does. Essentially this is the same as saying with John the Baptist, "He must increase, but I must decrease" (John 3:30). Our way of seeing, thinking, feeling, and understanding must be transformed into the way of Jesus. You and your life's circumstances are not outside the circle of friends that he invites into this transformation. He knows what you are going through. He knew it when you were formed in the womb. He knows every hair of your head, and he saw every moment of your life unfold before it did. He knows you are reading this right now. He knew from the beginning of time that you would go through this book, meet him here in a new way, and have the moment you are having right now. He also knows what you are about to do next, after you put this down. He *knows* you! Not only that, but he really *likes* you! Of course he loves you, but that can seem clichéd, and sometimes we don't let the meaning of that phrase really sink in. Do you know he likes you? You are a very likable person. Do you see yourself that way?

Moving forward, keep going. Even if you feel down, tired, or stressed, keep moving. When you don't think you have twenty minutes for a mindfulness exercise, just sit and do one minute. When you think you should be doing a Body Scan and only have time for a Sacramental Pause, do the Sacramental Pause. If you haven't practiced in four days, begin again anyway.

For right now, though, sit for a moment with the feeling of accomplishment that you have made it to the end of this book. You've made sacrifices, you've spent time with and for yourself and your relationship with God, and hopefully you've learned something new about yourself. My greatest prayer is that you've come to see yourself a bit more in the way God does and you feel a lighter burden as you move forward in your life. *His burden is light.* Instead of closing the book and rushing on to the next thing in your life, be present with yourself, sit a moment, and take a breath. May God bless you and fill you with his ever-present peace.

EXERCISE

Plant a Seed

Prepare a little pot with soil and the seeds of your favorite flower, fruit, or herb. As you prepare the pot, put in the soil, and plant the seed, do so in a mindful way. Pay attention to all of your senses as you do so. Give yourself the gift of being in the moment, experiencing this activity with your mind fully awake to what's happening now.

Cultivate this plant by watering it appropriately, and let it be a reminder to you of everything you have learned in this course. Keep it in a place that is visible so you can remember to practice mindfulness, return to your senses, and treat yourself with kindness and mercy.

Awareness of the present moment is something that will grow like this plant. You can't rush it or force it to be something it isn't, but you can gently nourish it and watch as it grows into what it is meant to be. Let your plant remind you of who you are.

APPENDIX I

Mindfulness: Buddhist or Catholic?

Catholic mindfulness is built on Catholic principles. In a world that often confuses new age practice with authentic Christian spirituality, some people may be concerned about the Buddhist roots of the concept and practice of mindfulness. It is true that Right Mindfulness is one of the steps for a Buddhist on the path to "enlightenment." Through a superficial analysis, there may be some cause for concern here, but let's look a little deeper.

First of all, it is helpful to understand what is essentially wrong with Buddhism for a Christian to believe. The most important reality of Christianity is the revelation of Jesus Christ as the Son of God, the second person of the Trinity. We are presented through this reality with the idea that God is a Trinity, both three and one. As God is the source of all creation, all being, all that is, his mysterious three-and-one nature is found in all that exists. Humanity itself is both a unity and a diversity of being. We are all one human family, ultimately made for the comm*union* of saints, while at the same time we are all individual human beings. A Buddhist, on the other hand, does not believe in both the unity and diversity of being. A Buddhist believes that only the unity is real, while the diversity is an illusion. The path to enlightenment for a Buddhist is the process of discovering that all sense of diversity is an illusion. This means that the self does not exist as a being separate from anyone else. It means that there is no God that exists separate from all being. Obviously this way of understanding the world is the complete opposite of a Christian worldview.

There are, however, many important insights into humanity developed by Buddhist thought. The path to enlightenment has eight steps, and while Christianity does not agree with its final destination, there are a number of steps that are consistent with the Christian sense of flourishing. Two other steps on the path to enlightenment, for example, are Right Speech and Right Action. We find here within the Buddhist teaching instructions for leading a good life that are very similar to what would be found in Catholic moral teaching.

Mindfulness as a Buddhist practice is simply the ability to stay focused on the present moment. Buddhist teachers have cultivated a specific understanding of the way the human mind works in light of this goal. While the idea of focusing on the present moment is found in Christian spirituality, the explicit understanding of the psychological process of paying attention to the present moment hasn't been developed much in those spiritual contexts. Mindfulness is a psychological process, not a spiritual one, so spiritual writers haven't been as concerned with the how of paying attention. If there is some concern about mindfulness somehow replacing authentic Christian spirituality, one has only to look past the surface to realize that it is not spiritual at all.

Mindfulness came to be known as a treatment protocol as the result of the work of Jon Kabat-Zinn, a researcher at the UMass Memorial Medical Center. In 1979 he launched Mindfulness-Based Stress Reduction (MBSR) as a treatment for chronic pain in his patients there. Kabat-Zinn had studied Zen meditation and Buddhist practice before that, and realized that he felt much more at peace as a result of his practice. He sought to introduce the benefits of his practice to a secular clinical population and thereby created MBSR.

While some practitioners try to connect MBSR to Buddhist philosophy, it is not an inherently Buddhist practice. In fact, Buddhist teachers can be very critical of mindfulness as it has been developed in our culture now, because it is detached from the full Buddhist path to enlightenment.

Kabat-Zinn realized, however, that as a result of his Buddhist beliefs, some of his mental practices brought peace to his racing mind. He wanted to bring that gift to his patients, and so he dissected the brain practice from the larger system and presented it as mindfulness.

Mindfulness Is Not Mind Emptiness

Some meditation practices lead you to try to empty your mind of all thought. Some people mistakenly believe the idea of mindfulness is the same as these ancient traditions of spiritual meditation from the non-Christian or Christian East. An important distinction between healthy mindfulness exercises and potentially misleading forms of spiritual meditation is found by simply paying attention to the word *mindfulness*. Where some of those non-Christian Eastern practices become dangerous is in the effort to empty the mind of all thought. Some religious traditions will use a mantra, some sound or word, or a name of a Hindu god to repeat over and over again, with the express purpose of emptying the mind of all thought and developing a kind of empty awareness. The subjective experience of this kind of meditation can be misleading. This is where these differing worldviews end up considering all thought, division, and even the sense of self as an illusion, because of what it feels like when one enters this state of emptiness.

Mindfulness is the exact opposite of this kind of practice! It is the effort to *fill* the mind with all that is around it. Mindfulness is waking up to reality, to the sights, sounds, tastes, feelings, smells, and thoughts that are happening in each moment. We seek to fill our minds with these realities during mindfulness exercise, not empty them of anything.

One caveat is that not all emptying is dangerous or unhealthy. In the Christian tradition there is also a sense of emptying that can be necessary on the path to union with God. The Greek word *kenosis* is often used to describe this Christian type of emptying; this idea is found in Scripture. Beyond that, sometimes the name of Jesus or a short prayer is used to help focus the mind to make space for God. There is an ancient Christian tradition of silent prayer called Hesychasm that is also similar. The experience of what happens in the interior of the body, mind, and soul can be different for everyone, and so explaining it can seem cumbersome or confusing at times, but the longer we sit with these mysteries, the deeper we can probe them.

Being Healthy Is Human

Christianity requires us not to be less open to the human experience, but to be more open. In 1989, when Pope Benedict was prefect for the Congregation for the Doctrine of the Faith, he wrote "Letter to the Bishops of the Catholic Church on Some Aspects of Christian Meditation." He was concerned about syncretism, or letting incongruent aspects of other religions mix with the practice of Catholicism. He clarified these issues for our contemporary culture. In this letter he made the important point of not throwing out the baby with the bathwater. First he made the distinction between health of the spirit and health of the body:

> Some physical exercises automatically produce a feeling of quiet and relaxation, pleasing sensations, perhaps even phenomena of light and of warmth, which resemble spiritual well-being. To take such feelings for the authentic consolations of the Holy Spirit would be a totally erroneous way of conceiving the spiritual life. Giving them a symbolic significance typical of the mystical experience, when the moral condition of the person concerned does not correspond to such an experience, would represent a kind of mental schizophrenia which could also lead to psychic disturbance and, at times, to moral deviations.[20]

Here he starts off with a significant warning about confusing physical sensations of peace with the assumption that all is well on a spiritual level. We know that spiritual well-being correlates with moral virtue. Sometimes feelings betray that reality and people can feel bad even though their actions are mostly good, or they can feel good even when their actions are mostly bad. We cannot confuse feelings with spiritual reality. Therefore no amount of practice, exercise, nutrition, spa treatments, or anything else that makes our bodies feel good can be an indication that we are spiritually close to God.

Pope Benedict goes on to say, however, that we can't disregard the importance of taking care of the body, or even using exercises that prepare the body and mind to enter into spiritual experiences:

That *does not mean that genuine practices of meditation which come from the Christian East and from the great non-Christian religions,* which prove attractive to the man of today who is divided and disoriented, *cannot constitute a suitable means* of helping the person who prays to come before God with an interior peace, even in the midst of external pressures.[21]

Non-Christian Eastern practices can be seen, according to Pope Benedict, as "suitable means" for preparing the mind to enter into a spiritual practice. So not only is mindfulness not an inherently Buddhist practice, as I've explained, but even if it were, we would still have good reason to learn how to practice it if it quiets the mind and helps us enter into prayer with interior peace. Some of the most brilliant Catholic spiritual writers have described the difficulty that comes from mental clutter, and the need to employ tools to help clear the way for the Holy Spirit to work. Cardinal Sarah says:

It is necessary to protect precious silence from all parasitical noise. The noise of our "ego," which never stops claiming its rights, plunging us into an excessive preoccupation with ourselves. The noise of our memory, which draws us toward the past, that of our recollections, or of our sins.[22]

Even St. Teresa of Ávila, a doctor of the church whose expertise was interior prayer, experienced at times "in my head many rushing rivers and . . . these waters are hurtling downward, and many little birds and whistling sounds."[23]

A Truly Catholic Practice

Ultimately mindfulness as a psychological practice works because it teaches us how to live in a mental and physiological state that is possible only when we have a neurological sense of being *safe*. The practice itself doesn't explain *why* we might feel safe. From the Buddhist perspective, we are safe because the ideas of safety and danger are illusions. Our individuality is an illusion, and dying is an illusion. Mindfulness could be practiced with this underlying philosophy, and in many places it is. If you are googling mindfulness and see results such as "illusion of self," "loss of self," or "ultimate unity with all being," you have found Buddhist mindfulness. Christianity proposes a different reality, another reason why we are ultimately safe.

Jesus tells us in Matthew 6:25, "do not be anxious about your life." It is not a suggestion or a hope—it is a command. He then goes on to explain that the birds and flowers are taken care of because of the Father's love. *The Father's love is key.* If we believe he loves us even more than the flowers and birds, then we can let go of tomorrow's troubles. This is why St. Paul tells us:

> Have no anxiety about anything, but in everything by prayer and supplication with thanksgiving let your requests be made known to God; and *the peace of God, which surpasses all understanding, will keep your hearts and minds in Christ Jesus.* (Philippians 4:6–7, emphasis added)

A strong tradition of spirituality has developed throughout Catholic history based on this idea. One of the most well-known examples, and a recommended book for further reading, is Fr.

Jean-Pierre de Caussade's *Abandonment to Divine Providence*. In it he describes how our entire lives can be given over to trusting the goodness of the Father, who loves us, guides us, and always gives us good things. This is a spirituality that is meant to include *all* things in life that we experience, especially the bad ones. Ultimately we never see reality unfolding as God does, and we don't know the full extent of the meaning or purpose of any event the way God does. This can be a very difficult point for many people, and probably one of the most common roadblocks to faith in Christ. If God is good and all-powerful and loves us, why does he let bad things happen to good people?

Mindfulness presupposes faith that God the Father is a *good* Father. Once, I sent out a flyer for a mindfulness course that mentioned "trustful surrender to God who loves us," which prompted a letter from an upset woman. She asked how she could be expected to practice mindfulness based on a God who loves her when he let her child die. There are no words to take away the horror and tragedy of an experience like this. However, these kinds of things are not outside the scope of what God knows, understands, and plans for. It is our way of thinking that needs to change—not God. It is precisely during these tragedies that our way of thinking has an opportunity to change in a way that someone who hasn't experienced that level of suffering can only imagine.

When we experience that kind of pain, we want it to go away immediately. We think of every possible way to make this happen, and the thought that God could make it go away but doesn't can be too difficult to bear. Therefore our minds come up with all kinds of arguments against God, against his goodness, his power, his love, his very existence. At times like these, it might make more sense to believe that God is angry, doesn't care about us, doesn't pay attention to us, or doesn't even exist.

"Why, God?" is the question we ask, but there is a different question. We might ask instead, "Where are you, God?" And if we can cry out to the Father, "Why have you abandoned me?" we just might hear, in between those sobs, the faint echo of our cries from the mouth of Jesus, who suffers with us.

It is not that God doesn't want to take away our suffering. It is that we have gotten to a place so far away that we must experience the suffering of purification in order to be close to God, like the fire that melts gold to remove its impurities. There is a certain element of mystery here, and no amount of words will ever adequately plumb its depths. However, if we tweak a bit the way we ask the question and look for a different answer, we might draw a lot closer to the healing insight at the heart of this mystery of suffering.

God never said life would be without suffering. If we need any evidence of this, we have only to look at the cross. If there's anyone the Father would have saved from suffering, it would have been his own son. As mysterious as this is, alleviating suffering isn't the way God proves his love. If he didn't do it when his own son begged him to "remove this cup" and cried out from the cross, "Why have you abandoned me?" there must be more to understand here.

Why let his son and himself go through such suffering? The answer can only be unrelenting love. God's love for us is why Jesus suffered the cross.

Here's a different way to understand suffering. Catholics are fond of the phrase "offer it up" to try to encourage one another in the midst of suffering. There might be some validity to the sentiment, but I think it is also sort of misleading (and many times unhelpful). If you've ever been the one suffering and someone has said, "Offer it up," you know what I'm talking about. This phrase has a sense of choice about it, as if you are choosing the suffering you are going through. We don't choose suffering; it is forced upon us. Sometimes we suffer as a direct result of our choices, but even then we certainly didn't choose the suffering. Because of original sin, we suffer. Because of the world, our fallen nature, or spiritual temptation, we suffer, and not by choice. The one who truly did have the freedom to offer it up is the one who didn't actually have to suffer. The one who did have a choice was Jesus. He didn't have original sin, and he didn't have to suffer.

This is the reality that can shift our thinking on the matter. Jesus, who did not have to suffer, chose to suffer because we suffer. He looked at us upon our crosses, and he said to himself, "If that's where you are, that's where I want to be." He was like us in "every respect, yet without sinning" (Hebrews 4:15). This means he suffered everything we suffer. He suffered the heartache of losing friends, of loved ones dying, of being misunderstood, even of being overworked (trying to get away from the crowds for a little time to himself but being pulled back in because of people's needs). Ultimately he allowed himself to go through the excruciating pain of suffering all this without the consolation of God's presence. "My God, my God, why have you abandoned me?" Why did Jesus go through that? Because we go through that. He knew he wasn't going to take away our suffering, so he joined us in it. God is really here for us. We can let go of our worries and trust him.

Again, the point is not to present something to you here that might fully take away your pain in times of great suffering. The point is to get you to think for a moment that if you are tempted to doubt the goodness or existence of the Father, maybe your doubt has more to do with the way you are thinking about it than the actual existence of the Creator of the universe. Maybe there's a different way to see things, in which even in the midst of this earth's greatest tragedies, God is still good.

The Pietà

This is the disposition that Mary had. She joined her son in his suffering, also choosing it for our sake, and in doing so presented a perfect model of faith for us. Michelangelo's *Pietà* shows us what this faith looks like. Mary, who raised the Son of God, witnessed countless miracles, hoped constantly in the salvation of the world through the kingship of her son, then watched as he was beaten and crucified, and held him lifeless, dead in her arms. What tragedy can you imagine that could more powerfully test one's faith in the goodness of God? She held her dead son in her arms and still trusted God's goodness and his plan. Besides the agony in the garden, I can't imagine another moment in all of human history more complex with the spectrum of human emotion at the deepest levels. "Now faith is the assurance of things hoped for, the conviction of things unseen" (Hebrews 11:1). This is faith.

That is the faith we aspire to. That is the faith we pray for and want to live our lives by. That is the faith that can change the way we actually live. This felt experience of faith can permeate the mundane activities we shuffle through every day of our lives. The depth of that faith can change the way we shop for groceries, take care of our kids, get stuck in traffic, manage finances, deal with coworkers, love our spouses, take care of leaky faucets, drink a beer or glass of wine with friends, meet strangers on the street or at the department store, spend time online or on our phones, pick out the clothes we wear, choose how to spend time with extended family, and countless other things. Our faith *should* affect these things—not just in trying to be more charitable, less greedy, more patient, and less selfish, but in letting "the peace of God, which passes all understanding . . . keep your hearts and minds in Christ Jesus" (Philippians 4:7).

God created us to have this peace at the deepest level—he intends for us to actually share in his peace. His peace changes everything.

APPENDIX II

Novena of Surrender to the Will of God

(adapted from a novena by Fr. Dolindo Ruotolo)

Begin by calling to mind the presence of God: "Ever-present God, here with me now, help me to be here with you." Let your mind rest in the present moment, in your presence here in this room encountering the presence of God. Let every problem and worry wash away in the flood of God's infinity. Know that he knows you, and he holds you in his loving embrace. Listen to his words as he speaks to you.

Day 1: Why do you confuse yourselves by worrying? Leave the care of your affairs to me and everything will be peaceful. I say to you in truth that every act of true, blind, complete surrender to me produces the effect that you desire and resolves all difficult situations. Even though you can't see how everything will turn out, I can, and you can trust me.

Day 2: "Surrender to me" means do not worry, do not be upset, and do not lose hope; it does not mean offering me a worried prayer asking me to follow along with your worry. To worry, to be nervous, and to desire to think about the consequences of anything is deeply against the surrender I require of you. It is like the confusion that children feel when they ask their mother for what they need and then try to take care of those needs themselves. Their childlike efforts get in their mother's way. Surrender means to peacefully close the eyes of the soul, to turn away from thoughts of tribulation, and to put yourself in my care.

Day 3: There is nothing I can't take care of when the soul, in so much spiritual and material need, turns to me, looks at me, and says to me, "You take care of it," then closes its eyes and rests. When you are in pain you pray for me to act, but you want me to act in the way you know. You do not turn everything over to me; instead, you want me to adapt to your limited ideas. You do not act as sick children who trust the doctor to heal you, but rather as sick people who tell the doctor how to do the healing. Do not act this way, but pray as I taught you in the Our Father: "Hallowed be thy name" (that is, may God be glorified in my need right now); "Thy kingdom come" (that is, let all that is in us and in the world be in accord with your kingdom); "Thy will be done on Earth as it is in Heaven" (that is, in our need, decide as you see fit for our temporal and eternal life). If you say to me truly, "Thy will be done," which is the same as saying, "You take care of it," I will intervene with all my omnipotence, and I will resolve the most difficult situations according to my infinite love and awareness of all things.

Day 4: You see evil growing instead of weakening? Don't worry; close your eyes and say to me with faith, "Thy will be done; you take care of it." I promise you that I will take care of it, and that I will intervene as does a doctor and I will accomplish miracles when they are needed. Do you see that the sick person is getting worse? Don't be upset, but close your eyes and say, "You take care of it." I say to you that I will take care of it, and that there is no medicine more powerful than my loving intervention. There is no evil stronger than my omnipotence or love. In this love, I promise you I will take care of everything.

Day 5: When I lead you on a path different from the one you see or expect, I will prepare you; I will carry you in my arms; I will take care of everything, and you will somehow find yourself, like children who have fallen asleep along the journey in their mother's arms, on the other side of the river. What troubles you and hurts you immensely is the misuse of your reason, your thoughts and worry, and your desire at all costs to deal with what afflicts you yourself. You do not understand everything the way I do. You did not create the sun, the moon, and the stars—I did. You do not keep the entire universe in existence—I do. Whatever it is you are afraid of or worried about, or that causes you to lose your peace, let it go. You can trust me.

Day 6: You are half-alive and agitated; you want to judge everything, direct everything, and see to everything, and you surrender to human strength, or worse—to certain people themselves, trusting more in their intervention. This is what hinders my words and my views. Oh how much I wish from you surrender, in order to help you, and how I suffer when I see you so agitated! Satan tries to do exactly this: to agitate you and to remove you from the knowledge of my protection and to throw you into the jaws of human initiative and self-dependency. Stop worrying because of what you see; stop trusting in the world to bring you peace. The world will never bring you peace. I am the only one who can give you peace. Even if I love you through human channels of my love and mercy, trust only in me, rest in me, and surrender to me in everything.

Day 7: The miracles of mercy I perform are in proportion to your full surrender to me and to your not thinking of yourself. When you give yourself to me as a child to a father, you give me full freedom to work in your life. I sow treasures of graces when you are in your deepest poverty. No scientist, no philosopher, and no saint has ever performed miracles or even great works on his or her own accord. He does divine works whosoever surrenders to God. So don't think about what worries you anymore, because your mind is limited and it is very hard for you to see evil where it is and to trust in me and to not think of yourself. Do this for all your needs, do this for everything, and you will see great continual silent miracles. I will take care of everything; I promise this to you.

Day 8: Rest now and let yourself be carried by the flowing current of my grace; close your eyes and do not think of your difficulties; turn your thoughts away from the future just as you would from temptation. I have made you in my image; you are precious to me. I have made you to feel immeasurable peace, but you will only find it if you look to me. Rest in me, believing in my goodness, and I promise you by my love that if you say, "You take care of it," I will take care of it all; I will console you, I will liberate you, and I will guide you.

Day 9: Pray always in readiness to surrender, and you will receive from it great peace and great rewards, even when I confer on you the grace of sacrifice, of repentance, and of love. Then what does suffering matter? It seems impossible to you? Close your eyes and say with all your soul, "Jesus, you take care of it." Do not be afraid; I will take care of all things and you will bless my name by humbling yourself. Remember this well: A thousand prayers cannot equal one single act of surrender. There is no prayer more effective than your trusting surrender to me.

End each day of the novena by repeating three times, "Jesus, I surrender myself to you; I trust you to take care of everything," and praying the following:

Prayer: Loving Father, I surrender to you today with all my heart and soul. Please come into my heart in a deeper way. I say yes to you today. I open all the secret places of my heart to you and say, "Come, Jesus." Jesus, you are the Lord of my whole life. I believe in you and receive you as my Lord and Savior. I hold nothing back from you. Holy Spirit, bring me to a deeper conversion to the person of Jesus Christ. I surrender all to you: my health, my family, my sexuality, my resources, occupation, skills, relation-ships, time management, successes, and failures. I release these things and let them go. I surrender my understanding of how things ought to be, my choice, and my will. I surrender to you the promises I have kept and the promises I have failed to keep. I surrender my weaknesses and strengths to you. I surrender my emotions, my fears, and my insecurities.

Holy Spirit, inspire my mind right now with whatever else I need to surrender.

[prayerful silence]

I especially surrender this to you.

Lord, I surrender my entire life to you—the past, the present, and the future. In sickness and in health, in life and in death, I belong to you.

Take, Lord, and receive all my freedom, my memory, my intellect, and my will. You have given me all that I have and I return everything now to you. Dispose of me according to your will. Give me only your love and your grace, for with this I am rich enough and have no more to ask.

Amen.

NOTES

1. Mark Williams and Danny Penman, *Mindfulness: An Eight-Week Plan for Finding Peace in a Frantic World* (Emmaus, Penn.: Rodale, 2012), pp. 37–43.

2. Brother Lawrence of the Resurrection, *The Practice of the Presence of God* (New York: Doubleday, 1977), p. 64.

3. Fr. Jacques Philippe, *Searching for and Maintaining Peace* (New York: Society of Saint Paul, 2002), p. 11.

4. Williams and Penman, *Mindfulness*, pp. 91–92.

5. St. Thérèse of Lisieux, *Story of a Soul: The Autobiography of St. Thérèse of Lisieux*, 3rd ed., trans. John Clarke, OCD (Washington, D.C.: ICS Publications, 1996) p. 37.

6. St. Thérèse of Lisieux, *Story of a Soul*, p. 165.

7. Philippe, *Searching for and Maintaining Peace,* p. 6.

8. R. S. Friedman and J. Forster, "The Effects of Promotion and Prevention Cues on Creativity," *Journal of Personality and Social Psychology* 81 (December 2001), pp. 1001–1013.

9. Karol Wojtyla, *Love and Responsibility* (San Francisco: Ignatius Press, 1993), pp. 201–206.

10. St. John Paul II, General Audience: "Humans Are Spiritual and Corporeal Beings," April 16, 1986.

11. *Diary of Saint Maria Faustina Kowalska: Divine Mercy in My Soul* (Stockbridge, Mass.: Marian Press, 2010), p . 392.

12. Jean-Pierre de Caussade, *Abandonment to Divine Providence* (North Palm Beach, Fla.: Beacon Publishing, 2017), pp. 25–26, emphasis added.

13. Nancy Bardacke, *Mindful Birthing: Training the Mind, Body, and Heart for Childbirth and Beyond* (New York: HarperOne, 2012).

14. Marie Mongan, Hypnobirthing: *A Natural Approach to Safer, Easier, More Comfortable Birthing*, 4th ed. (Deerfield Beach, Fla.: HCI, 2015).

15. Robert Cardinal Sarah, *The Power of Silence: Against the Dictatorship of Noise* (San Francisco: Ignatius Press, 2017), pp. 84–85.

16. Ibid.

17. Ibid.

18. Martin Seligman, *Flourish: A Visionary New Understanding of Happiness and Well-Being* (New York: Atria Books, 2012).

19. Josemaría Escrivá, *The Way* (New York: Image Books, 2006), no. 191, no. 206.

20. Joseph Ratzinger, "Letter to the Bishops of the Catholic Church on Some Aspects of Christian Meditation," 28; October 15, 1989.

21. Ibid., emphasis added.

22. Sarah, *The Power of Silence*, p. 85.

23. *Interior Castle*, Fourth Mansion, chapter 1, No. 10.

ABOUT THE AUTHOR

DR. GREGORY BOTTARO is the director of the Catholic-Psych Institute and the developer of the Catholic Mindfulness online course. Before getting his doctorate, he spent four years living as a Franciscan friar, serving the poor in the tradition of St. Francis. He ultimately discerned a call to pursue family life. Six years after leaving New York City as a friar, Dr. Bottaro returned as a psychologist. His aim was fundamentally the same—to serve. Instead of serving those suffering material poverty, he now seeks to serve those with psychological needs. This is his first book.

INTRODUCTION TO
CATHOLIC MINDFULNESS

Dr. Greg Bottaro teaches an eight-week online course called "Introduction to Catholic Mindfulness." You can sign up for this course and begin at any time.

Sign up now at **www.catholicmindfulness.com.**

Use coupon code "mindfulcatholic" for 20 percent off the cost of the course!

Learn how to experience greater peace in your life through video, with other students, in a way that will help you meet your goals!

What's included:

- Live recording from Dr. Bottaro's classroom for each week of the course
- Audio exercises to follow along with and enhance your understanding and practice
- Collaborative interaction with other students taking the course
- More personal anecdotes, clinical stories, and live interaction